# Blend It Splendid

# Blend It Splendid

The Natural Foods Blender Book

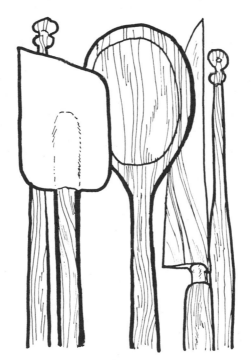

by
Stan and Floss Dworkin

**RODALE PRESS, INC. BOOK DIVISION**
Emmaus, Pennsylvania 18049

ISBN 0-87857-062-4

Library of Congress Catalogue No. 72-93638

FIRST PRINTING—June 1973
PB-147

PRINTED IN THE U.S.A.
on recycled paper

Also by the Dworkins:

BAKE YOUR OWN BREAD
AND BE HEALTHIER

# CONTENTS

# PREFACE

## LET ME TELL YOU HOW WE EAT
Stan Dworkin

It's appropriate that I write the Preface, because, while Floss does the baking and an occasional fruit salad, I do all the cooking. And I spend less time in the kitchen than anyone I know.

To give you an example, in the SOUP chapter you'll find a recipe for Borscht. Our recipe is adapted from a recipe given us by a Russian lady. To prepare it, she takes half a day; with the blender, I take half an hour.

"Nothing to excess" is the Apollonian mean—and it is very much the way we construct our diet. Floss and I don't depend on any one "miracle" food or vitamin to keep us well and well nourished, but rather try to balance our eating, getting our food values from natural, wholesome foods, as well as dietary supplements.

We eat no pork, very little beef or lamb (and that mostly liver or kidney), some poultry and some fish.

We no longer eat any tuna or swordfish, once quite important in our diet—now our main fish is turbot, caught in less polluted Greenland waters. As for shrimp, we are aware that all shellfish can accumulate pollutants. Our shrimp—available from Shiloh Farms, frozen—comes from cleaner waters around Iceland. We feel shrimp is too good a food to drop completely. But you must know where they come from.

We drink a good deal of skim milk (reconstituted from

noninstant nonfat milk powder), and eat yoghurt, cottage cheese, hard cheese, and eggs.

We eat legumes, especially soybeans.

We eat large amounts of nuts and seeds—much more than you'll find in most diets.

We eat whole grain cereals and whole grain, home baked breads (see our *Bake Your own Bread and Be Healthier*, Holt, Rinehart, and Winston)—whole wheat, whole rye, whole corn, wheat germ.

But most of all we eat vegetables: broccoli, cauliflower, spinach, zucchini, carrots, Swiss chard, celery, cabbage, dark green lettuces, tomatoes, cucumbers, potatoes, brown rice, turnips, parsnips, beets, butternut squash, and so on, depending on the season.

We eat a lot of fruits: oranges daily, melons rich in vitamin A, a lot of apples, and seasonal stuff, too.

We use hardly any hot spices at all. I was once kept on a completely spice-free diet for a number of years, and we both lost our taste for hot stuff. Now that we can have spices, we still use very little of them.

We buy herbs by the pound—not the half ounce. The Gypsies have always used herbs for health as well as flavoring, and we like to think they're right. For us, herbs take the place of a lot of salt and pepper.

Our salt shakers are full of the Herb and Vegetable Salts you'll find in Chapter 5.

We cook with a little wine, and we drink some wine.

We take eating yeast—especially when we need a concentrated food in a hurry.

We take vitamins and food supplements—liver tablets when we don't have liver, dolomite for calcium, and so on.

We avoid saturated fats. Heart disease is still an outrageously large killer on the home front. We trim the fat off any meat, even kidney, and skin our chicken. We have some *un*saturated fat every day (usually as salad dressing) and that helps. The saturated fat is the reason we avoid cream and whole milk.

Our usual unsaturated fat is cold-pressed oil. Cold pressing leaves the nutrients intact. (For more on cold-pressed versus commercial oils see page 87.)

Also to protect our hearts, we use as little salt as we can. And what salt we use is either sea salt or unrefined mined salt (whenever, in recipes, we call for sea salt, you can substitute unrefined mined salt). Of course, salt is salt and it can cause circulation problems. But, in addition to this danger, supermarket salts are loaded with dessicants to keep them free-flowing and nonclumping. We go the unrefined and sea-salt route to avoid the chemicals, but if your taste buds can be happy without any salt at all, drop the salt from the recipe.

In our kitchen, no food is cooked a long time. Which is, in part, where the blender comes into our lives. Not that everything we eat comes from the blender—far from it. Most of our meals are vegetables cut up well in the Chinese style and then cooked very briefly just to soften the cell walls and make the nutrients more available. But the blender does help us to achieve minimal cooking with many dishes.

We have found the blender important in designing our diet. With a little thought, you will, too.

We eat no canned food at all. Canned food is often salted, and it is cooked at high enough temperatures to destroy enzymes, vitamins, and minerals—and that is without even considering the argument that the metal of the cans gets into your food.

We eat very little frozen food—though we use some frozen fruits when the fresh are out of season. In fact, we try to eat as little processed food of any kind as we can get away with.

"Nothing to excess" does not mean "Everything in moderation." We don't hold with nutritionists who say that small amounts of poisons won't hurt us. All the poisons that we eat must be processed in the body, just like all the wholesome food. The poisons go through our systems, leaving their destructive marks just as the wholesome foods go through, building our bodies.

We won't eat the paraffin coating on cucumbers (and sometimes bell peppers).

We avoid saturated fats.

We won't bake a bread with white flour unless we add wheat germ to replace some of the B vitamins that have been removed.

We won't eat white sugar in any amount, no matter how small. (Our sweeteners are honey, blackstrap molasses, and maple syrup.) We never *buy* any breads, cakes, candy, cookies, crackers, or pastry because they are made with refined sugar and white flour and hard fats and chemicals. We try not to eat sprays, even though the President's Council on Nutrition says the world can not be fed without them.

How do we avoid sprays? We belong to a health food co-op here in New York City, The Greenhouse Association. The Greenhouse does some of its own testing of the food it orders, so we can be certain, at least in part, that what we are eating is wholesome.

When we buy our produce elsewhere, we wash thoroughly in hot water, and then sometimes peel.

Another whole class of foods we avoid is Standard of Identity foods. You'll be seeing mentions of Standard of

Identity foods and this is a good place to explain. According to a law passed in the thirties and amended since, the makers of certain foods do not have to list the ingredients of their products on their labels. This group includes such foods as bread, salad dressings and mayonnaise, ketchup, ice cream, cheese and cheese products, cocoa products (chocolate), jams and jellies, soda pop, spaghetti and macaroni, certain canned foods, and many others. Which means that for about 20 percent of the food eaten in this country, consumers have no specific idea of what they are eating. Of course, you could write to the Department of Health, Education, and Welfare and get a copy of the Standard of Identity for the foods you were curious about. But even then, you won't know exactly what is in the food, because the federal government has established broad outlines of ingredients (including long lists of chemicals) from which the manufacturer can choose and still fall within the limits of the Standard of Identity.

What do we do? We don't eat or drink any Standard of Identity food. In fact, many of the recipes in this book are alternatives we have invented or adapted to permit us to get off the Standard of Identity not-so-merry-go-round.

We are happy and we are healthy. When we weren't so healthy, we weren't so happy. But our good health didn't come from diet alone. You cannot be healthy, no matter how good your diet, if you don't exercise, and if you don't make some kind of treaty with the world immediately around you.

We are happy in our work.

We folk dance vigorously, we bicycle, we camp, we walk, we practice a little yoga, we exercise.

Healthy eating, and an awareness of where it fits into your life, is a good beginning.

# INTRODUCTION
## USING YOUR BLENDER

Your blender is a tool, and to get maximum efficiency from it, you have to know its powers and its limitations.

First of all, read the instruction manual that comes with your blender. Most manufacturers don't know fully what their blenders will do, and so that booklet is not gospel, but it can give you some ideas of special features and limitations of your machine.

Don't assume that you can (or would want to) do everything the booklet says you can do, and don't assume that everything the booklet says you can't do is beyond you.

But there are a few things you cannot do with a blender, generally because the blades move at too high a speed to work enough air into the food. You can't whip cream—at least not so that it really seems like whipped cream. You can thicken cream, but the blender blades move too fast for whipping (if you're not careful, you can try for whipped cream and wind up with butter). You can't mash potatoes —when moved at that speed, potatoes become viscous and sticky, not mashed. Egg whites get thick but not stiff. However, there are so many things you *can* do with your blender that we feel you can't complain.

Here are a few words on the care and feeding of your machine.

CLEANING: It's very important to clean your blender from meal to meal. That is, don't let the milk you reconstitute in the morning sit around until the evening. Once processed, foods can spoil, go rancid, quite quickly. If you are not using your blender again immediately, do clean it well.

However, do not wash out your blender between operations in the same or consecutive recipes.

We take our blender container completely apart to clean. The kinds with a removable base are quite superior to the one-piece models in that respect. If you can't remove the bottom, you will have a hard time cleaning out stuff like cheese spreads or mashed dates. To clean this 1-piece kind of machine, rinse out the container as well as you can by hand (be careful when putting your hand into the blender container—the blades, even still, can cut), then half fill it with hot water and a little detergent and process at high speed until the blades and bottom are clean.

We can't emphasize too much how important cleaning is —especially if you use your blender only occasionally.

MAINTENANCE: You probably cannot maintain your blender motor—and most of them are very difficult to get at. If the motor smells as if something is burning, then something is likely to be burning, and it will require a return to the maker—hopefully under the warranty. However, follow the instruction manual's maintenance hints. While the manufacturer doesn't know the limitations of the blender's use, he does know how the motor works.

Try to use your blender heavily during your first days of ownership. Many department stores will exchange within the first week without any real questions, and then you don't even have to go to an authorized service center. Don't hesitate to exercise the waranty or guarantee. You are entitled to a well-functioning machine.

SAFETY: Your blender is a dangerous machine, like so many household appliances. However, only a minimum of care and caution is required to run it safely. UNDER NO CIRCUMSTANCES PUT YOUR FINGERS INSIDE THE CONTAINER WITH THE MOTOR RUNNING. This may seem obvious, but it bears stating and restating. Don't put hard (wood or metal) objects into the blender container with the motor running. If you wish to use the rubber spatula we recommend, first shut off the machine. Otherwise, you'll chop up your spatula, or worse yet you'll break a blade. If you smell anything burning, stop and investigate Don't be stubborn and burn out your blender.

SPEEDS: With every recipe, we have given an appropriate speed. However, the blender should be used at the lowest speed possible for the job. If you find that your blender will process stuff into an appropriate texture at a lower speed, then make a note in the recipe and reduce the speed next time. The blender generates a good deal of heat in processing your foods. That heat is destructive of certain vitamins. The lower the speed the less heat—the less heat the more vitamins.

Conversely, if you find that your machine won't give you the right texture at the speed we've indicated, then increase the speed. Not all blenders are created equal.

WHAT ELSE?: We use one object in connection with the blender—a rubber spatula with a wooden handle. It is made by Rubbermaid and cost, at last purchasing, twenty-nine cents. Spatulas do get used up, even with great care. The blender blades, even still, cut into the rubber. But we don't mind spending the money, because a spatula is so helpful in scraping stuff out of the blender (and out of measuring cups into the blender), and for scraping stuff down off the sides of the blender and onto the blades.

There is one other thing you need—imagination. Because it is our hope that these are not just recipes and ideas to file and reuse, but that they will lead you to inventing your own uses for the blender, lead you to healthier recipes and ideas of your own.

# 1

# SOUPS

Blenders are for soups and soups are for blenders. There is no other group of foods that lend themselves so well to blender cooking. To keep maximum nutrition, foods should be cooked as little as possible. Heat destroys some vitamins, minerals and enzymes. The less you cook a food the more of these necessities remain in the finished product. Your blender allows you to cook a soup minimally, yet still have it seem cooked when you bring it to the table; in fact, a blender allows you to have *raw* soup—especially important for vitamins A and C.

The one long-cooking exception in this chapter is the recipe for Basic Chicken Stock. While there is some food value left in this stock after it has been cooked for 45 minutes, we don't count on it for nutrition; we consider the stock just a rich "water." What we put into the stock supplies the heat-sensitive nutrients.

In those recipes that use stock, the flavor of the soup depends largely on the flavor of the stock used as the base. A rich stock will lend lots of flavor—a thin one will need reinforcing with additional seasonings. Do taste your soups before they are finished processing in the blender: you may want to add seasonings. Also, many of the recipes in this section were standardized with organically grown vegetables from our health food co-op. Organically grown spinach tastes fuller, at least to our palates—regular super-market vegetables may need more flavoring. So don't bring a recipe to the table on faith—taste and adjust to your own preferences.

There are a few special techniques particular to soups:

Our blender will process a full 5 cups without splashing—if yours won't, you'll want to divide some of the recipes in half and process each half separately;

A vegetable that has been cooked (or one that's soft to begin with, such as mushrooms) chops coarsely very quickly—so, if you want coarse vegetables in a soup, just flick the machine on and off very briefly;

For a cream soup, put the milk powder in last;

When you add milk powder to a soup for creaming, the mixture has a slight tendency to foam—leave room in your blender;

The milk we use is noninstant powdered nonfat milk. The *noninstant* means that you must shake it vigorously or use a blender to mix it as it doesn't dissolve like the Carnation-type instant. Noninstant powdered milk is at present available only in health food stores (or through mail order houses), but it's worth getting for its superior flavor and higher vitamin, enzyme, mineral, and protein content;

Generally speaking, soups should be processed at low speed—even when you're looking for something creamy. Other ideas or problems, particular to specific recipes, will come up in the recipes.

For just as much flavor with less salt, substitute equal amounts of any one of the special Salts given in Chapter 5 for the sea salt called for in the recipe.

# ALMOST INSTANT SOUPS

We're quite proud of these four soups, because they are our own invention. We know Lipton's invented instant soup a while before us, but, because they won't give us their recipes, we had to invent them all over again.

These are convenience soups. They are made with dried ingredients and so are nutritionally inferior to soups made with fresh ingredients, but they still have a lot of nourishment and they are great for that day when you didn't shop or couldn't get anything fresh.

Almost Instant Soups are made up in advance and will keep in your closet for months without refrigeration even though they do not contain the preservatives or chemical additives of the commercial instant soups. We hope you read the labels of everything you buy before you buy it. If you do, you've read the labels of those packaged instant soups and know the number of chemicals they contain. Here's a way to get rid of the chemicals, but still have dry soup in the closet, ready for emergencies.

Why are they called "Almost Instant" you ask? For truth-in-labeling: how can you call any soup that takes 5 to 15 minutes to cook "instant"?

## ALMOST INSTANT VEGETABLE SOUP

½ cup dried lentils
½ cup dried green peas
½ cup dried yellow peas
½ cup dried onion flakes
1 cup dried carrots
2 tablespoons sea salt
1 teaspoon dill seed
¼ teaspoon black pepper
¼ cup dried dill weed (see p. 216)
1 teaspoon ground bay leaf (see p. 216)
2 tablespoons raw wheat germ
¼ cup seaweed (kelp or dulse)

Blend the ingredients at medium speed, 1 cup at a time, until like meal. Pour the ground ingredients into a large bowl and stir well, mixing until uniform. Spoon into a large-mouthed jar with a tight-fitting lid.

To serve, add 3 heaping tablespoons to 2 cups of water, bring to a boil, and simmer for 5 minutes more. Do not allow to boil over.

If you haven't ground the beans and peas well enough, the large chunks will be uncooked at the end of 5 minutes.

## ALMOST INSTANT FISH SOUP

This recipe is made with dried salt cod (and it must really be dry). Dry salt fish has few vitamins remaining by the time you buy it, but it still remains a source of protein, as are the soy beans. Do not allow the soup to boil over.

> ¼ *pound dry salt cod*
> ½ *cup dried soybeans*
> ½ *cup dried lentils*
> ¼ *cup dry parsley (see p. 216)*
> 1 *tablespoon dill seeds*
> ½ *teaspoon ground bay leaf (see p. 216)*
> ¼ *teaspoon paprika*
> ¼ *cup dried onion flakes*
> 2 *tablespoons raw wheat germ*

Cut the salt cod into 1-inch squares and blend at low speed a few at a time. As the fish is chopped, pour the fish fibers into a large bowl. Blender grind the soybeans into chunks —not a fine powder—and dump into the same bowl. Pour the rest of the ingredients into the blender and blend until they have a meal-like consistency. Pour this mixture into the bowl and stir until uniform. Spoon into a large-mouthed jar that seals tightly. Refrigerate this one: the fish never dries out enough to store safely in a closet for more than a few weeks.
To serve, add 2 heaping tablespoons to 2 cups of water and bring to the boil, then simmer for 10 minutes more, stirring once or twice.

## ALMOST INSTANT THREE SEAWEED SOUP

This is a soup you can make only if you have access to an Oriental food store. You can sometimes find one or two kinds of seaweed in a health food store, but the variety of seaweeds, the daikon (dried radish strips), and the shrimp are not to be found outside of an Oriental specialty shop. The shrimp we use here are the heavier, denser kind, but the transparent ones will do as well—though they are more expensive. This nutritious soup contains iodine and all the trace minerals of the ocean.

*1 ounce dried shrimp*
*½ ounce dulse*
*½ ounce laver*
*1 ounce daikon*
*2 ounces soybeans*
*few dashes black pepper*
*½ teaspoon ground bay leaf (see p. 216)*
*1 teaspoon sea salt*
*1 tablespoon granulated kelp*

Blend the shrimp briefly until they are coarsely chunked, then pour into a bowl. Break up the dulse and laver, blend them fine, and pour into the bowl. Blend the daikon into largish bits, and the soybeans quite small. There is no need to blend the rest of the ingredients, just add them to the bowl. Stir until the mixture is uniform. Spoon into a large-mouthed jar, and store in a closet. This recipe will keep for months.

To prepare, add 3 heaping tablespoons to 2 cups of water, bring to a boil, and then simmer for 10 minutes more, stirring once or twice. Do not allow to boil over—which this soup will do given the least chance.

## ALMOST INSTANT MUSHROOM-BARLEY SOUP

This is the simplest and most delicious of the almost instant soups, but prone to boiling over.

*1½ ounces dried mushrooms*
*¾ cup medium barley (dry)*
*3 tablespoons onion powder*
*2 rounded tablespoons Dill Salt (see p. 135)*
*3 tablespoons dried dill weed (see p. 216)*

At high speed, blender grind the mushrooms for a few seconds; pour into a mixing bowl. Grind the barley for half a minute—or until it looks like coarse sand—then add to the mushrooms. Measure the remaining ingredients into the same bowl and stir well until the mixture is uniform. Spoon into a large-mouthed jar, and store in a closet.

To cook, add 3 tablespoons of the mixture to 2 cups of water, bring to the boil, and then simmer for an additional 15 minutes.

# HOT SOUPS

Here is a warning about blending hot soups: soups direct from the stove are often too hot for the safety of your equipment. While the heat is unlikely to break the glass of a blender container, it is likely to melt the lubricant of the blade mechanism—leading to loud screeching from the machine and repair bills. So, when no additional cooling liquid is called for in the recipe, do allow 10 to 15 minutes for the soup to cool before you pour it into your blender. If the soup needs reheating, pour it back into the original pot—except for cream soups, which should be reheated in the top of a double boiler to keep the milk from scorching.

## BASIC CHICKEN STOCK

For any recipe in this book calling for soup stock, you can use this recipe (or the recipe for Vegetable Stock on page 18). However, don't think this is only a stock; it's also a rich and delicious Chicken Soup, usable as is with no additions. You can substitute chicken parts for the whole chicken, but whether you use whole chicken or parts, be sure you trim off all the skin and any loose fat. Chicken fat is 30 percent saturated fat, and no good for your system.

> 2½-pound chicken
> 4 quarts hot water (total)
> ½ pound onions

*2 medium carrots*
*2 large stalks celery*
*1 tablespoon sea salt*
*few dashes black pepper*
*1 tablespoon dried parsley (see p. 216)*
*2 pinches thyme*
*1 teaspoon leaf sage*
*1 teaspoon granulated kelp*

Trim the skin and fat from a 2½-pound chicken, cut into pieces, and put into a large pot with 2½ quarts of the water, and turn the flame on high. Cut the onions into chunks and put them into the blender container with 2 more cups of hot water. Blender chop coarsely by turning the machine on and off briefly. Pour onions and water into the soup pot. Using 2 more cups of hot water each time repeat with the carrots and celery, separately, first cutting them into 1-inch pieces. This brings us to a total of 4 quarts of water when all the vegetables are in the pot. Add the salt, pepper, parsley, thyme, sage, and kelp, and bring to a boil. Reduce the flame to medium and cook, uncovered, for an additional 40 to 45 minutes, tasting for additional seasoning after about 30 minutes. Remove the chicken and eat it, but leave all the vegetables in the stock.
Even with lean or trimmed chicken, this soup will contain a good deal of chicken fat, so be sure you skim the fat off before you use the stock. The easiest way of removing the fat from any chicken or meat soup is to put the pot in the refrigerator and allow to cool; the fat will solidify on the surface and can be conveniently removed.
Chicken stock will keep for about 4 to 5 days in the refrigerator—if you never take it out. If you take the pot out and put it back, out and back, 3 days is the probable limit before it will turn bad (it is a perfect medium for bacteria). So, if you don't expect to use all the stock at once, pour the unneeded portion into plastic containers and freeze until wanted.
Yield: about 3½ quarts.

## VEGETABLE STOCK

Here's a stock so thick and rich that you can if you wish strain off some of the vegetables and eat them separately or mix them with an egg for a broiled croquette.
We cook this stock so short a time that much of the vitamins are left intact.

> 1 pound white or yellow turnips
> 4 quarts water (total)
> 1 pound potatoes
> 1 pound onions
> 1 pound carrots
> 2 stalks celery
> 1 rounded teaspoon ground bay leaf (see p. 216)
> 1 teaspoon ground sage
> 1 teaspoon leaf thyme
> 2 tablespoons Vegetable Salt (see p. 137)
> 2 tablespoons tamari soy sauce

Wash and trim, but do not peel, the turnips. Cut into ½-inch chunks and blender chop in 2 batches, each batch with 2 cups of water. As the turnips are chopped, pour off with the water into a large soup pot and turn on the heat to medium-high. Wash and trim the potatoes, but do not peel, cut into 1-inch pieces and blend covered with 3 cups of water. Add to the pot. Peel and chunk the onions, and blender chop in 2 batches, each with 2 cups of water. Add to the pot. Wash and trim, but do not peel, the carrots; cut into 1-inch pieces and blender chop with 3 cups of water. Add to the pot. Wash the celery, cut into 1-inch pieces, and blender chop with 2 cups of water. Add to the pot with the herbs and salt. Allow to come to a boil and reduce the flame to a simmering heat. Taste after 15 minutes, then add soy sauce to taste. Cook for 5 minutes more (a total of 20 minutes).
(You have added a total of 4 quarts of water with the vegetables.)
Yield: about 4 quarts.

## ASPARAGUS PUREE

The flavor of this soup is subtle and delightful, because we cook the asparagus for only a few minutes. If there are those in your family who won't eat asparagus without a high-calorie cream sauce, try this on them.

> *2 cups cold Vegetable Stock (see facing page)*
> *4 large stalks asparagus*
> *¼ teaspoon fennel seed*

Measure the cold stock into your blender. Wash the asparagus and trim off only the dry ends. Cut into 1-inch pieces and add to the stock with the fennel seeds. Blend at medium speed until quite smooth. Pour into a saucepan, heat over a medium flame until your mixture reaches a boil, then reduce the heat and simmer for 5 minutes only. Serve hot or cold.
Yield: 3 cups.

## KIDNEY BEAN SOUP

Substitute soybeans or black beans in this hearty and delicious soup, and it's just as good.

> *1 pound dry kidney beans*
> *6 cups water*
> *1 small onion*
> *2 medium stalks celery*
> *2 teaspoons sea salt*
> *dash pepper*
> *3 tablespoons vegetable oil*
> *2 tablespoons raw wheat germ*
> *raw bean sprouts for garnish*

Wash beans in hot tap water. Soak them overnight in about 6 cups of hot water. Next day, place over medium-high heat and add 1 small onion (about 1½-inch diameter), peeled and quartered, the celery, cut or broken into 2-inch

pieces, the sea salt, a dash of pepper, and the vegetable oil. When the pot comes to the boil, reduce the heat to medium and cook for about 3 hours, until the beans are edible—soft but not mushy. When done, shut off the flame and allow to cool for about 15 minutes, then stir in 2 tablespoons raw wheat germ. This recipe is too large to go into the blender all at once, so spoon half the mixture into the blender and process at low speed until smooth. Repeat with the second half. Reheat gently in the same pot. Garnish each serving with a sprinkling of any raw, home-sprouted bean sprouts.
Yield: 4 large servings.

## ROUGH CARROT SOUP

This is *not* a recipe for carrot puree but a recipe for a soup with *chunks* (small chunks, we grant) of carrot in it. So, remember, flick your blender on and off *briefly* in the final stage. The flavor of this soup depends very much on the flavor of the carrots you use. We use organically-grown carrots flown in from California, and they are sweet and flavorful. Do try to get tasty carrots.

> 2 tablespoons liquid vegetable oil
> ¾ pound carrots
> 4 cups cold stock (see p. 16 or p. 18)
> 1 scallion
> 1 tablespoon dry parsley (see p. 216)
> 2 pinches leaf thyme
> salt and pepper

Pour 2 tablespoons of oil into a large skillet. Wash and slice carrots about ¼-inch thick, and sear (that is, sauté at highest heat) in the skillet, with the cover on, for 5 minutes. Add stock, scallion (in 1-inch pieces), parsley, thyme, and salt and pepper if needed—and allow this mixture to come to the boil. Boil at medium heat for 10 minutes with the cover off. Allow to cool for 10 to 15 minutes and pour into the blender container. Blend very briefly; the texture of the soup demands it.
Yield: 4 to 5 cups.

## CELERY SOUP

This is so simple and quick that you can have Celery Soup in 15 minutes from getting the urge.

>    5 medium stalks celery
>    1 small onion (about 1½-inch diameter)
>    ½ teaspoon sea salt
>    ½ teaspoon celery seeds
>    2 cups stock (see p. 16 or p. 18)

Cut the celery into 1 inch pieces, quarter the onion, and put both into the blender container with the soup stock. Chop coarsely by flicking the switch on and off briefly once or twice at low speed. Pour into a pot with the salt and the celery seeds, bring to the boil, then boil at medium heat for 5 minutes. Allow to cool for 5 minutes, then return the mixture to the blender, processing until smooth. Reheat in the same pot, or put the soup into the refrigerator, for this soup is equally delicious hot or cold.
This recipe yields only 3 cups, so you may want to double it. If so, blend half the celery and onion at a time, but cook it all together.

## EGGPLANT SOUP

Don't knock it till you've tried it.

>    1 large eggplant
>    1 tablespoon sea salt
>    2 tablespoons vegetable oil
>    1 large onion
>    1 teaspoon dill seed
>    3 cups stock (see p. 16 or p. 18)
>    ⅛-¼ teaspoon mace
>    sea salt and pepper

Prepare the eggplant 1 hour in advance: trim and quarter, but do not peel, the eggplant, and cut it into ¼-inch slices. Place the slices in a large bowl, and pour over them 1 tablespoon salt. Cover with a dish smaller than the bowl and weight down the dish with something weighing about 5 pounds. (A bronze bookend would do.) The salt causes the eggplant to excrete a brownish liquid—it's this liquid that so often makes eggplant taste bitter.

After an hour, remove the weight and the dish. In the bowl, rinse the eggplant with cold water (you don't want to eat all that salt). Now, pick up a small handful of eggplant slices and, over the sink, squeeze them until no more liquid comes out. (We know it sounds oddball, but it does work.) Put the squeezed eggplant aside; repeat until all the eggplant is squeezed.

Measure the oil into a large skillet. Chop the onions coarsely by hand, and brown in the skillet with the dill seed. Do *brown* the onions. Add eggplant, mace, and a dash of salt and pepper. Cook, stirring occasionally, until the eggplant is soft—about 10 minutes. Shut off the heat and add the cold stock. Pour into the blender and blend till smooth. Taste for additional salt. If this soup is too thick, add more stock to thin it. Reheat in the same skillet. Yield: about 4 servings.

## TOMATO SOUP

This basic recipe is for a hot soup. For raw tomato soups eaten cold, see Tomato-Yoghurt Soup and Gazpacho on pages 33 and 34. It is not necessary to get expensive hothouse tomatoes for this recipe. Those squishy overripe tomatoes behind the produce counter are just as good—if not better. The brief cooking makes all the flavors great. Don't use canned tomatoes: in fact, don't use canned food. Fresh stuff is amazingly simple to prepare, and superior in flavor, texture, and nutrition.

*2 tablespoons vegetable oil*
*8 large tomatoes*
*1 tablespoon dried basil (see p. 216)*
*1 teaspoon fennel seeds*
*sea salt*

Measure the oil into a large skillet. Cut the tomatoes into chunks and put in the skillet, along with the rest of the ingredients, including a sprinkling of sea salt. Cover, and cook at highest temperature for 7 minutes. Allow to cool for 5 minutes. Pour into the blender, process at low for a few seconds. Reheat in the same skillet.
Yield: a quart.

# BISQUES

Bisques were originally seafood soups, thick and with the seafood chopped into bits. Now, any thick soup with the ingredients chopped up can be called a bisque—which qualifies most of the soups in this chapter. However, the three recipes that follow seem to us the most bisque-like.

## FISH BISQUE

The fish we most often use for this recipe is turbot fillet. We get it frozen solid from the fish department of our nearby supermarket, and stick it right in the freezer until we're ready to use it. It comes from Greenland waters via Japanese fishing boats, which, we understand, freeze the fish right on board. However, any frozen fish fillets will do, even those prepacked ones. If you wonder why we use frozen in preference to fresh fish, it's because the frozen fish are usually fresher. This isn't as paradoxical as it sounds. Many fish are frozen where they are caught, nowadays, meaning that they are, when you defrost them, only a day or so old. The so-called fresh fish in our markets are usually much older than that—unless you are lucky enough to get that day's catch right off the docks in a fishing port. However, you can use fresh if you wish.

> 1 large onion
> 2 tablespoons vegetable oil
> 1 teaspoon dill seed
> ½ teaspoon sea salt
> 1-1¼ pounds hard-frozen fish fillets
> 2 cups hot water
> 2 very heaping tablespoons noninstant milk powder

Cut the onion into coarse pieces and sauté in a large oiled skillet, with the dill seed and sea salt, for 10 to 15 minutes over a medium flame (until almost scorched). During this time, cut the frozen fish into ½ to ¾ inch cubes. You may need to saw with a serrated knife if the fish is very thick. Add the fish cubes to the skillet and sauté, stirring frequently, until the fish is just done, 5 to 8 minutes. (Don't overcook! The reason frozen fish has such a poor reputation is that people tend to defrost it completely before cooking—which leaves it watery—and then overcook it. Frozen fish should always be cooked still partly frozen. There should be no raw sports, but the fish should just barely flake apart.)
Spoon half the fish-onion mixture into the blender with 1 cup of hot water and 1 very heaping tablespoon noninstant milk powder. Blend for a few seconds only, at low speed. Reserve, and repeat with the other half of the fish, another cup of hot water, and another heaping tablespoon of milk powder.
Serve immediately.
Yield: about 4 cups.

## SHRIMP BISQUE

We like to cook some extra shrimp whenever we have it for dinner, so as to have cold shrimp for salads and this easy Bisque. By the way, we hope you cook your shrimp as little as possible. It's easy to ruin shrimp by overcooking.

We boil the water (with a bit of bay leaf, dill seed, celery seed, and sea salt), drop the shrimp in, then let the water come back to the boil and cook for only about 1 minute more. The shrimp, unless they are very large, get done through, but they are still full of flavor.

>  2 cups hot water
>  2 very heaping tablespoons noninstant dry
>     milk powder
>  1 tablespoon whole rye flour
>  1 teaspoon sea salt
>  2 tablespoons vegetable oil
>  1/8 teaspoon black pepper
>  1 1/2 tablespoons white wine
>  2/3 cup cooked, peeled shrimp
>  paprika for garnish

In the blender, mix the water and milk powder. Blend in the flour, salt, oil, pepper, and wine (we use dry vermouth). Add the shrimp and flick the machine on and off at low speed until chopped.
To serve, heat in the top of a double boiler, or very carefully in a pot directly on the heat. Garnish with a sprinkling of paprika over each bowl.
Yield: 3 cups.

## POOR MAN'S THICK BISQUE

You don't have to be poor to make this bisquelike soup, but it is economical. The recipe is made with the water the potatoes were cooked in. And we hope this isn't the only use you make of this potato water. It's quite rich in minerals and some vitamins—as well as being tasty. Potato water, or any vegetable water, can be used in bread baking, soup stocks, stews, anywhere that water is called for except in sweet things. Remember, vegetable water is usually salted, so don't add salt without tasting. If you make this recipe with plain water, add 1 teaspoon of one of the flavored Salts in chapter 5.

1 cup potato water
2 very heaping tablespoons noninstant dry
    milk powder
2 cups cooked potatoes (with skins)
½ teaspoon sea salt
1 ounce wine
pepper
2 teaspoons dried dill weed (see p. 216)
fresh bean sprouts for garnish

Mix the potato water and milk powder in the blender. Add the potatoes, salt, wine (the cap of most new blenders is a 2-ounce measure), a few dashes pepper, and the dill weed. Blend until smooth.
Garnish with a small handful of fresh raw bean sprouts.
Yield: 3 servings.

# CREAM SOUPS

Cream soups were usually thought of in the segment of society in which we were raised as sophisticated things you ate at soignée soirées. Well, they are sophisticated, though simple to prepare. But they are more, too. Cream soups are good sources of milk protein, for kids and adults both.

Of course, the words "Cream Soups" are a euphemism here, because we don't use cream in any of them—cream is much too high in saturated fat. We use noninstant spray-dried nonfat powdered milk—from the health food co-op. If you want to use the lower protein, lower calcium, instant powdered milk, substitute 1/3 cup of milk powder for every very heaping tablespoon in the recipe. Bottled skim milk is okay too, but it is overpriced.

You'll sometimes find it impossible to substitute whole milk or bottled skim milk for the powdered, because we use soup stock as our liquid.

For the most part, adults should avoid whole milk; it can lead the way to upper-respiratory diseases and is too rich in butterfat.

## CREAM OF ALMOND SOUP

Usually, recipes for almond dishes call for blanching. That's just to remove the skin (part of our national passion for making everything white), and it's not necessary. If you have no almonds, try the recipe with an equal amount of peanuts or walnuts—or any other nuts that come to hand. It's possible to make a rather fine nut flour with your blender, but we don't want that here. Rather, try to grind the almonds to a coarse meal. Almonds are rather hard nuts and easier to keep coarse than peanuts or walnuts.

> *¼ pound almond nutmeats*
> *3 cups stock (see p. 16 or p. 18)*
> *1 scallion*
> *1 stalk celery*
> *¼-½ teaspoon ground mace*
> *1 cup cold water*
> *2 very heaping tablespoons noninstant milk powder*
> *sea salt*

Blender grind the nutmeats to a coarse meal. Put this into a pot with the soup stock, the scallion and celery (each cut into 1-inch pieces), and the mace. The amount of mace you use depends on how well you like mace—explore by tasting to be certain. Bring to a boil and continue to boil, over a medium flame, for 10 minutes. Turn the flame off and add 1 cup of very cold water. Pour the mixture into the blender and add the milk powder. Blend for a moment at low speed. Taste for salt or more mace.
Yield: about 4 cups.

## CREAM OF POTATO SOUP

This soup starts out thin but thickens as you reheat it. It has more protein and more calcium than a quart of milk. The recipe calls for *raw* wheat germ. Wheat germ contains an oil (all grain germs do); this oil does not have a !ong shelf life. To extend the shelf life, wheat germ is often toasted. Toasting, in essence, "kills" the germ and destroys the vitamin E. Raw wheat germ is often cheaper and always (when fresh) a better food, but it must be refrigerated or the oil will turn rancid. However, even toasted wheat germ is rich in B vitamins.

> *1 small raw onion*
> *1 cup cooked potato, with skins*
> *2 cups potato water*
> *4 very heaping tablespoons noninstant milk powder*
> *¼ teaspoon sea salt*
> *1 tablespoon raw wheat germ*
> *1 tablespoon dry parsley flakes (see p. 216)*
> *dash pepper*

Cut the onion into quarters and the potatoes into 1-inch chunks, then dump all the ingredients into the blender and process at low speed until smooth.
To serve, reheat in the top of a double boiler, or carefully in a pot.
Yield: about 3½ cups.

## MUSHROOM CHEESE SOUP

We're proud of this recipe because it's so simple, so quick, and so good. This is a party soup that you can prepare in minutes, and yet serve to any company. If you haven't any mushrooms, this makes a delicious cheese soup, but it really shines with the mushrooms.

> *3 cups soup stock (see p. 16 or p. 18)*
> *6 ounces uncolored cheddar cheese*
> *2 very heaping tablespoons noninstant milk powder*
> *2 ounces fresh raw mushrooms*

Warm the stock, but not so hot you can't put a finger in it. Put the warmed stock into the blender. Cube the cheese and add it and the milk powder. Process at low speed until smooth. If your mushrooms are small, add them whole to the container; if they are large, half or quarter them and put them into the container. Flick the blender on and off very briefly once or twice. Nothing disappears quite as quickly as mushrooms, and the soup will be disappointing if you can't chew on the mushroom bits.

To serve, heat carefully to avoid scorching.

Yield: almost 5 cups.

## CREAM OF CARROT SOUP

This soup is hot stuff, and not for children or for people who must eliminate spices from their diet. Of course, no one should eat a lot of spicy foods—at least no one raised in our culture. But anyone with a normal digestive tract should be able to handle small amounts of spices occasionally with no difficulty. But that is "small amounts" and "occasionally." For kids, delete the curry powder.

> *¾ pound fresh carrots*
> *1 small onion*
> *2 tablespoons vegetable oil*
> *3½ cups soup stock (see p. 16 or p. 18)*
> *⅛ teaspoon ground bay leaf (see p. 216)*
> *2 teaspoons curry powder*
> *½ teaspoon sea salt*
> *2 very heaping tablespoons noninstant milk powder*

Wash well but do not peel the carrots. Cut them into ¼-inch slices. Thin slice the onion. Sear the onions and carrots in an oiled skillet for 7 minutes. Reduce the heat to medium and add the soup stock, bay leaf, curry powder, and sea salt. Bring to a boil and allow to boil for 5 minutes. Cool for 10 minutes, then pour into the blender. Add the milk powder and process at low speed until smooth.

Reheat in the same skillet, carefully, to avoid scorching. Cream of Carrot Soup is also delicious cold.

Yield: 4 or 5 servings.

## TOMATO-CHEDDAR SOUP

This recipe calls for uncolored cheddar cheese. Naturally, cheddar cheese has an off-white color, similar to that of cream. However, most of the cheddar sold in this country is yellow, and it is yellow from dye. All the so-called American cheese is cheddar, processed to soften and smooth it, and then dyed yellow. Most supermarkets now offer you a choice of colored and natural cheeses. Choose natural.

This is a winter soup, very hearty and very filling. It is perfect for a meal where the only other items on the menu are home-baked whole wheat bread and a salad.

> 1 Tomato Soup recipe (see p. 22)
> ½ pound sharp uncolored cheddar cheese
> 1 cup water
> 1 very heaping tablespoon noninstant milk powder
> 2 dashes nutmeg

Prepare the Tomato Soup recipe on page 22 and reserve. Make up the milk powder with water and reserve. Cut the cheddar into 1-inch cubes and grate in the blender. Add the Tomato Soup and blend until smooth. Add the milk and blend again until uniform.

Yield: 5 cups.

# COLD SOUPS

Cold soups are among our favorites. For the most part they require no cooking, are quick to prepare (requiring little or no planning), are delicate of flavor, and are real eye-openers for company. For cold soups you have to be a little more careful in your shopping: the overripe tomatoes that were fine for the hot Tomato Soup would taste over-ripe here, and a very strong onion gets no chance to be tamed down.

## AVOCADO SOUP

The manager of the produce department at our supermarket and we are very happy with one another; one reason
is that we will take those soft avocados that other shoppers
squeeze and bypass. Those shoppers are silly. We get these
softer avocados at a much reduced price, and they have a
superior flavor. Most people think an avocado has to be
very firm to slice into salads. Like so many other fruits,
avocados are shipped into our markets before they are fully
ripe. So, if all you've ever tasted are the rather bland and
underripe avocados, go back to the produce department
and look for the ones that have been reduced in price.
They are sweet and delicious—as you'll find out if you use
them in this unusual soup.
We use yoghurt in this recipe—home-made, of course; it's
so easy and inexpensive that way.

> 2 medium avocados
> ½ cup yoghurt (see p. 215)
> 2 medium cloves garlic
> 1 small onion
> 2 cups cold water
> 2 very heaping tablespoons noninstant milk powder

Spoon the meat out of the avocado shells (save the seeds
for planting) into your blender. Peel the garlic and onion.
Quarter the onion and add it and the rest of the ingredients. Blend until quite smooth.
Yield: 4 cups.

## BORSCHT

Here is a soup like your great grandmother used to make
in the old country. In fact, this recipe is adapted from the
recipe of a lady who used to make it in the old country—
Russia. There are fair borschts available commercially—if
you don't mind a few chemicals—but they are not nearly
as good, nor as provocative of extravagant praise.

Please note that we make this exotic soup in less than half an hour.

> 1 pound beets (weighed without greens)
> 4 cups water
> 2 small lemons
> 3 eggs
> 1 teaspoon sea salt
> 1 tablespoon honey

Wash, peel and trim the beets, cut into chunks, and blender chop at high speed in 2 batches, each with 2 cups of water. When chopped, pour off beets and water into a pot with a cover. Place over a medium flame. Peel and pit the lemons, then liquify at high speed. When the beet and water mixture reaches the boil, add the lemon. Reduce the heat and simmer for 15 minutes, cover off, or until the beets are cooked crisply. Remove from the heat and allow to cool for 10 minutes. In a bowl, mix together the eggs, salt, and honey. Dribble this mixture into the beets slowly, stirring well, until all the egg mix is in. Stir again. The Borscht should be a pinkish color and thicker—from the eggs.
Serve cold or hot.
Yield: about 1 quart.

## COLD CUCUMBER AND YOGHURT SOUP

If you use the long green cukes for this soup you'll have to peel the skins off, unless you grow them yourself or get them from a farmer before they are waxed for the city markets. For that is what happens to cukes that have to travel a long way—they get coated with paraffin; and our digestive tracts can't digest paraffin. However, Kirby pickles —the pale-green, bumpy cukes that are used to make sour pickles—can be used skin and all, once they are scrubbed clean. Kirbies aren't waxed.
This is a great hot-weather recipe.

1 pound cucumbers
½ cup home-made yoghurt (see p. 215)
½ teaspoon sea salt
1 teaspoon granulated kelp
1 teaspoon dried dill weed (see p. 216)
1 teaspoon raw wheat germ
dash nutmeg

Trim the hard ends and any bad spots from your cukes and cut them into 1-inch pieces. With the motor at medium speed, drop the pieces a few at a time into the blender, until they are liquified, then add the remaining ingredients and process until smooth.
This recipe yields only 3 cups, but it is easy to double.

## COLD TOMATO-YOGHURT SOUP

There is no easier recipe in the book.

1 pound raw tomatoes
½ cup yoghurt (see p. 215)
1 teaspoon granulated kelp

Wash the tomatoes in hot water, trim off the cores, and cut into chunks. (If you use Italian or plum tomatoes, just wash and cut them in half.) Drop the chunks a few at a time through the opening in the cover of your blender and process at medium speed until smooth. Add the yoghurt and kelp and blend for a few more seconds until a uniform color.
Yield: 3 cups.

## COLD CHERRY SOUP

The Scandinavians love cold fruit soups, and who can blame them. They tend to be sweeter than most soups, and rather unusual in flavor, but really delicious. Make sure this one is quite cold before you serve it. We use frozen, pitted sweet cherries to make this soup, because the idea of pitting all those cherries turns us off completely. If you insist on pitting your own, start with a pound of cherries to get the 2 cups.

> ¼ *lemon*
> 2 *cups pitted sweet cherries*
> 1¾ *cups water*
> ¼ *cup honey*
> ¼ *cup sherry*
> ¼ *teaspoon ground cinnamon*

Pit the lemon and blender grate the whole piece including skin and pulp. Put all the remaining ingredients in a pot with the lemon, bring the mixture to the boil, and then simmer for 5 minutes. Refrigerate. When cool, blend at low speed for a few seconds only. There will still be nice little chewy cherry bits. Refrigerate until ready to serve.
Yield: 4 small servings.

## GAZPACHO

This is a very ethnic Spanish soup that varies from district to district and from region to region. This particular recipe comes from the healthier region.
We use cold-pressed oil in many of our *uncooked* foods because it has a bit of vitamin E left in, and no solvent. Most supermarket oils have some vitamin E, but also residues of the solvent used in the processing to get rid of the pulp.

> 1½ *pounds ripe tomatoes*
> 2 *large leaves chicory or escarole*
> 1 *small onion*
> *splash vinegar*
> 2 *tablespoons cold-pressed vegetable oil*
> 1 *large clove garlic*
> ½ *teaspoon sea salt*
> ⅛ *teaspoon pepper*
> ⅛ *teaspoon paprika*
> 1 *tablespoon raw wheat germ*

Wash and core the tomatoes, then chunk them and drop them into the blender a few at a time until liquified. Feed in the leaves of chicory or escarole. Quarter the onion and blend it, then add the rest of the ingredients to the blender and process at medium speed until smooth. Refrigerate.

The traditional way of serving Gazpacho is with a garnish of chopped cucumber or green pepper and with an ice cube floating in the middle. While I approve of the vegetables, the ice cube is a bit much unless you live in the tropics.

Yield: nearly 5 cups.

## GREEN SOUP

This is a soup very high in vitamin A—which means that it should be eaten immediately and not stored in the refrigerator. Vitamin A decomposes on contact with air, so, the sooner eaten, the more A. If you use ingredients very cold from the refrigerator, the soup will be cold enough to eat immediately.

> *½ pound tomatoes*
> *½ pound cucumbers*
> *1 ounce watercress, both leaves and stalks*
> *a few spinach stalks and leaves*
> *1 cup very cold water*
> *1 rounded tablespoon kelp*
> *1 teaspoon dried basil (see p. 216)*
> *½ teaspoon dill weed (see p. 216)*
> *1 cup fresh yoghurt (see p. 215)*

Wash and core the tomatoes, cut them into chunks, and drop them into the blender a few at a time until liquified. Wash, trim, and cut the cucumbers into 1-inch chunks (see page 32 for the story on cukes), and feed them one at a time into the tomato liquid, at medium speed. Wash the watercress well and add while the machine is going. Wash the spinach well and feed the leaves in one at a time. Add the rest of the ingredients and blend at medium speed for a few more seconds. Serve immediately.

Yield: about 4 cups.

## TOSSED SALAD SOUP

Gazpacho is called Spanish salad soup, and this is *our* salad soup. It came to us that salads don't have to be eaten with a fork, and this was the delicious result. As with the Green Soup, serve as quickly as you can. This is the longest recipe in this chapter; that's simply because our salads are always more complicated than our soups.

> 3 large escarole leaves
> 1 large stalk celery
> 2 tablespoons cold-pressed vegetable oil
> splash vinegar
> ½ small lemon
> ½ cup cold water
> 1 small onion
> 1 medium cucumber
> 2 cups tomato chunks
> 1 teaspoon dried basil (see p. 216)
> ½ teaspoon powdered garlic
> ¼ teaspoon granulated kelp
> ¼ teaspoon sea salt
> 1 tablespoon raw wheat germ

Tear the escarole to pieces, cut the celery in 1-inch chunks, and place in the blender. Add the oil, vinegar, the lemon (seeded, but with the skin), and the water. Blend at medium speed until everything is in bits. Peel the onion, cut into quarters, and add to the blender. Scrub the cuke and cut it into 1-inch pieces; add to the mixture with the tomato chunks. Blend until smooth. Add the remaining ingredients and blend for a few more seconds. This will never blend as smooth as puree, so don't try.
Yield: 4 cups.

## MOCK VICHYSSOISE

The reason this is mock and not real vichyssoise is that the real stuff is made with leeks and this is made with scallions. Our produce man said, when asked for leeks, "Thirty-nine cents for one *this* big." *This* was a distance of about an inch between thumb and forefinger. It seems that leeks are always expensive nowadays, and scallions are often cheap. If you can afford leeks, substitute 2 leeks for the scallions and put them into the skillet *with* the onion. Do not remove the greens from the scallions; most of the good is in the green. Tamari is a kind of aged soy sauce; it is salty, so the recipe calls for no additional salt.

*1 large onion*
*2 tablespoons vegetable oil*
*1 bunch scallions*
*2 cups soup stock (see p. 16 or p. 18)*
*1 pound new potatoes (with the skins)*
*small handful fresh parsley*
*⅛ teaspoon grated nutmeg*
*few dashes pepper*
*few drops tamari soy sauce*
*1 cup cold stock for cooling*
*2 heaping tablespoons noninstant milk powder*

Thin slice or blender chop and drain the onions and sauté them in an oiled skillet until transparent. Cut the scallions into 1-inch lengths and add to the skillet and cook briefly. Add 2 cups of stock, a pound of thin-sliced new potatoes (raw and with their skins on), the parsley, the nutmeg, and pepper. Cook until the potatoes are just done. Cool with 1 cup of cold stock and pour everything into the blender. Add the tamari and milk powder, and blend it all until quite smooth. If this is too thick, thin with more cold stock. Refrigerate until quite cold. (Don't tell anyone, but it's delicious hot, too.)
Yield: almost 5 cups.

# MAIN COURSES
# AND
# SIDE DISHES

What's the difference between a main course and a side dish? Mainly, the amount you eat of it. Certainly you can't say that meat and fish dishes are main courses and vegetables are side dishes. If you do, we'll disagree most enthusiastically (enthusiastically because we like nothing better than to show heavy meat eaters how good, how delicious, and how main so many vegetable dishes can be). So, eat 12 Four Root Pancakes and that is most certainly a main course; eat one or two Broiled Chicken Croquettes and that is a side dish. Go on, be revolutionary, eat a meal that's mostly or entirely vegetable dishes, with only a tiny bit of chicken for animal protein. You might find you like it.

We listened to a doctor speaking on the radio, promoting his diet book, and he gave what he called a test diet— *it had meat at all three meals.* Now that is one strange diet, especially when the body's need for the complete protein that animal protein supplies is really quite small, and can be provided by fish, poultry, cheeses, eggs, milk, and, much more cheaply, through soybeans. Don't misunderstand us; we're not saying all at once and completely, drop all animal protein from your diet. That's not the way we live. But we are saying that the body's need for animal protein is much smaller than what we've been brought up to think, and a much healthier and better balanced diet would be achieved by reducing the amount of animal protein in your diet, and increasing the amount of vegetables you eat. We've done it, and have never been so healthy or happy in our lives. There is a problem with main courses in the blender. Or shouldn't we admit that there can be any problems with healthy blender cooking? At any rate, the blender holds no more than a quart or so—at least, not without spraying it over your kitchen—so that you can't make a main course for 10 people with one filling of the blender. Of course, with dishes like our Stews, you fill the blender several times to make a main course for about 6. So, main or side dish, most of the recipes here will serve several people— even several hungry people.
Let's talk techniques.

CHOPPING. In chopping you end up with discernible bits. The best way to do this in a blender is to put liquid in with the vegetable you are chopping. Cover the food with water, turn the blender on low speed, and turn it off quickly. With practice you will get to know the *sound* your machine makes while there are still big chunks and the sound it makes when everything is chopped. For finer chunks, blend a little longer, for coarser, a little less. If there are one or two pieces left unchopped, don't throw everything back into the blender—either cut them by hand, or pull them out to use elsewhere, or just ignore them and leave them in with the smaller bits. There's no law that says that everything has to have the same texture. In fact, variations in texture are very interesting, as the Orientals have known for millennia. Once chopped, pour the water and vegetables through a colander sitting in a bowl, and allow to drain well. This blender water, left over after chopping, is now quite rich and should be saved for soups or drinks or baking.

GRINDING. In grinding you blend everything down to a kind of puree. To achieve this, cut the vegetable into 1-inch pieces and feed the pieces through the hole in the blender cap, a few at a time. Often, the first few pieces only chop, and it is not until several pieces are in that true grinding is achieved. Often, your blender will have as difficult a time processing too little as too much. For large amounts, your blender may not be able to process all the vegetable at one go and may require a scraping out before grinding the rest of the vegetable.

GRINDING MEAT AND FISH. The process is much the same, except that meat and chicken tend to be tougher than vegetables, even hard vegetables such as turnips or winter squash. So, if your blender isn't sturdy enough for the job, pass it by. And remember, your blender does not chop meat: it makes the same kind of puree of meat, chicken, and fish, as it does of vegetables.

# STEWS

Can we call it a "stew" if it doesn't stew on the stove for a long while? Well, we think we can, and so here are four Stew recipes that are fairly quick, and a great deal of fun. They require a number of ingredients, and in that way they are like traditional stews, but there is nothing traditional about their flavors, or about the amount of nutrients left after cooking.

## CABBAGE STEW

The vegetables in this recipe are called for in cups of cubed vegetable. Remember that in order to chop food in the blender, you have to first cut it into inch chunks, or smaller. Don't core the cabbage—that's good for you too. It's not necessary to let the vegetables drain well, but do reserve the water, reusing the same water for each chopping. By the time you finish chopping, it is very rich and flavorful water, and gives the stew a head start. Also, don't forget how full of nutrients it is.

> 2 cups potato chunks
> 2 cups onion chunks
> 1 cup carrot chunks
> ½ medium cabbage
> 2 tablespoons vegetable oil
> 1 tablespoon sea salt
> dash pepper
> 1 tablespoon dried sage (see p. 216)
> 2 pinches thyme
> ¼ teaspoon ground bay leaf (see p. 216)
> 2 teaspoons ground coriander
> 2 cups blender water

Scrub, but do not peel, the potatoes and cut into chunks. Blender chop, covered with water (see page 9). Pour into a strainer set in a bowl, to retrieve the water. Peel and cut up the onions, blender chop, and drain in the same colander. Wash, but do not peel, the carrots, and repeat using the same water. Wash the cabbage and cut into inchish chunks. It will take 2 or 3 choppings to get it all. Keep reusing the same water. Pour about 2 tablespoons vegetable oil into a large pot (about 4 quarts), and turn the flame to highest heat. Scrape the drained vegetables from the colander into the pot, and add salt, pepper, sage, thyme (those are rather large pinches), bay, and coriander. Sear for 5 to 7 minutes, uncovered, stirring once or twice. Add 2 cups of vegetable water, bring to boil, and cook for about 10 minutes. Taste.
Yield: 6 servings.

## QUICK GIZZARD STEW

This dish is made with gizzards because they are tasty, good for you, and cheap. Gizzards are dense and can be hard on your blender. But what stew could be faster.

> 1½ pounds fresh chicken gizzards
> 2 medium onions
> 2 medium carrots
> 2 medium stalks celery
> 2 tablespoons vegetable oil
> 2 teaspoons sea salt
> dash or 2 pepper
> 1 tablespoon dried sage (see p. 216)
> 2 pinches thyme
> ½ teaspoon ground bay leaf (see p. 216)
> 1 tablespoon dried parsley (see p. 216)
> about 3 cups blender water

Wash and quarter the gizzards, then cover with water and blender chop coarsely. Drain in a colander set in a bowl, reserving the water. Peel the onions, cut into chunks, and cover with the same water. Chop coarsely and drain. Wash, but do not peel, the carrots, cut into 1-inch chunks, chop, and drain. Wash the celery, and repeat, saving the water for later use. Pour the vegetable oil into the bottom of a large pot (about 4 quarts), and turn the heat on high. Scrape all the processed ingredients from the colander into the pot and add the salt, pepper, sage, thyme (2 large pinches), bay, and parsley. Sear for about 5 minutes (until gizzards are done), stirring occasionally. Add 3 cups blender water. (If you didn't end up with 3 cups, add a little plain water.) Bring to a boil, then shut off, taste for additional seasoning, and eat.

For an option, you could add 2 cups cooked potatoes, cubed, just before adding the water.

Yield: 6 servings.

## VEGETABLE STEW

If you dilute this recipe at the end with 2 quarts of water, it can be a rich vegetable soup or stock. But we like it best this way—concentrated.

*1 cup tomato chunks*
*2 medium onions*
*2 medium carrots*
*1 large stalk celery*
*1 medium parsnip*
*1 medium white turnip*
*1 green pepper*
*2 tablespoons vegetable oil*
*2 teaspoons sea salt*
*dash or 2 pepper*
*1 tablespoon dried sage (see p. 216)*
*2 good pinches thyme*
*¼ teaspoon ground bay leaf*
*1 tablespoon dried parsley (see p. 216)*
*1 tablespoon dried basil (see p. 216)*
*2 cups blender water*

Wash the tomatoes, and cut into 1-inch chunks, and reserve. Peel the onions, cut into chunks, and blender chop, covered with water. Pour into a colander set in a bowl, and reuse the water. Repeat with the carrots, celery, parsnip, turnip, and green pepper, scrubbing the vegetables, but not peeling them, and reusing the same water. Pour the vegetable oil into a large pot and put in the tomato chunks. Sear for 2 minutes at highest heat to express the tomato liquid, then scrape in the chopped vegetables, add the seasoning, and sear the mixture for 10 minutes more, stirring twice. Add 2 cups blender water and boil for about 8 minutes. If it tastes done, serve immediately. If not, boil for another few minutes.
Yield: 6 servings.

## VEGETABLE STEW, TOO

You may have to chop the onions in 2 batches. There is no need to add extra liquid to this stew, so save the blender water for another use.

> 2 pounds onions
> 2 large cloves garlic
> 2 tablespoons vegetable oil
> ½ pound tomatoes
> 2 pounds raw potatoes
> 1 pound zucchini
> 1 teaspoon sea salt
> ⅛ teaspoon pepper
> 1 tablespoon dried parsley (see p. 216)

Peel and blender chop the onions and garlic together, covered with water. Drain in a colander set in a bowl. Pour vegetable oil into the bottom of a large pot. Scrape in the drained onion and garlic and sauté until transparent, over medium heat. Hand chop the tomatoes into smallish chunks and reserve. Wash and blender chop the raw, unpeeled potatoes, covered with water, and drain. When the onions are clear, add the tomatoes and cook briefly, until some juice is expressed. Then add the potatoes and cook until almost done, about 15 minutes over the same medium flame. Meanwhile, blender chop the zucchini, covered with water, and drain. After the potatoes have cooked for about 15 minutes, add the zucchini and the seasonings and cook for another 5-10 minutes, uncovered, until the zucchini is al dente.
Yield: 4 servings.

# PASTA

Noodles are nice, especially if you make them yourself. Then you know just what goes into them and how and under what conditions they are made.

The two recipes that follow are for green noodles, but you could, using these two as guides, make squash noodles, or carrot noodles, or turnip noodles, or noodles from any other vegetable that will chop up very fine in the blender. So, experiment.

There are two main problems with making noodles: where do you roll them out, and where do you put them to dry once they are rolled out. First of all, you don't have to roll out all the dough at once. In fact, while it does give one a sense of power, it is rather difficult to roll out the whole batch and get it thin and even.

We roll out a bit at a time with a rolling pin directly on our old enamel kitchen table. You could do the same on a Formica-top table, or on any kneading board. Once the noodles are cut (we use a noodle cutter for that, but a sharp knife will do, cutting off one long noodle at a time), they can be draped over waxed paper draped over the backs of chairs in the Italian method until they are dry. But don't let them all dry. Noodles are best when eaten fresh, so cook some while they're still soft.

When the noodles are thoroughly dry, store them in a plastic bag in a closet—there's no need to refrigerate them. Your whole-grain noodles won't come quite as thin as white noodles.

## WHOLE WHEAT SPINACH NOODLES

This recipe is made with fresh, not packaged spinach, which means that it should have the hard bottoms still on when you buy it. (You know, of course, that spinach grows in a bunch, like lettuce, with the stems joined at the bottom.) This makes the spinach a little easier to handle, and also preserves a little of the moisture. Weigh the spinach with the knuckles on.

> *3 eggs*
> *1 pound fresh spinach*
> *4 cups whole wheat flour (plus a little more for*
> *flouring the board)*

Break the eggs into the blender. Trim off the hard bottoms, then wash the spinach and drain well, but do not towel dry. Start the blender going at low speed and feed the spinach leaves and stems in one at a time, through the hole in the blender cap. DO NOT PUT YOUR FINGERS INSIDE THE CONTAINER. When the mixture begins to get thick, increase the speed. When all the spinach is blended into the eggs, scrape the mixture into a bowl.

Add the flour 1 cup at a time. The 4-cup figure is approximate. You must finish with a dough that is dry enough to roll, but one that is moist enough to roll thin; so, add as much of the 4 cups of flour as needed. When you have enough flour, work by hand until you have a cohesive ball. Divide the dough into pieces, sprinkle your board or table with a little flour, and roll out each piece (the rolled-out pieces can be reserved on wax paper until cutting). While rolling, turn the flattening dough over after every few rolls—this will help prevent sticking. Don't be afraid to apply light flourings to the board and rolling pin. When all the pieces are rolled as thin as you can get them, cut into noodles with a noodle cutter or a sharp knife, or shape them into squares to make Ravioli (see page 48). Dry over the back of a chair or on wax paper anywhere.

Cooking time depends on the thickness of your noodles. Wet noodles will cook up in about 10 minutes, dry noodles will want longer.

Yield: about 1½ pounds of dry noodles.

## SOY–WHEAT GERM–BROCCOLI NOODLES

This combination is high in protein and B vitamins. We use only the stems of the broccoli because we like to use the flowers for other dishes, but you can use the whole broccoli, stems and flowers, if you like.

> 3 eggs
> ½ pound broccoli stems
> ½ teaspoon sea salt
> 1 teaspoon granulated kelp
> 1 cup soy flour
> ½ cup raw wheat germ
> 1¾ cups unbleached white flour (plus a little for
>     flouring the board)

Break the eggs into the blender container. Wash the broccoli well and cut into ½-inch pieces. Drop the pieces through the hole in the blender cover, with the motor going at high speed, until well blended. Add the salt and kelp and blend in briefly. Scrape out into a bowl.

Mix in the soy flour, and then the wheat germ. Stir in the white flour half at a time. As with the previous noodle recipe, work in only enough flour to stop the dough from sticking and permit rolling. When you have enough flour, work by hand until you have a cohesive ball. Roll out, cut, and dry as on page 46.

Fresh, boil for 12 to 15 minutes; dry, boil longer. Cooking time depends on the thickness of your noodles.

Yield: about 1¼ pounds dry.

## RAVIOLI

Ravioli are stuffed pasta, and either of the two recipes for noodles can be used to make them. But instead of cutting the rolled-out dough into thin strips, as for noodles, you cut the rolled-out dough into large thin squares.

Make up either noodle recipe. Divide the dough into 4 equal pieces, and roll out as thin as possible into 4 roughly equal squares. Lay a square on your working surface, and, starting at the top, drop teaspoonfuls of filling (see below) at equal distances, about 1 to 1½ inches apart, like putting checkers on a checkerboard. Do another row; then another, until the square is covered with evenly spaced globs of filling. Wet your finger in plain water and run it down and across the rows and around the outside, wetting the dough well (this is what will glue the two layers of dough together). Lay another square over the first, gently, and press horizontally and vertically over where you have wet it. Run a finger over the joints several times to make certain all is well glued, then cut between the rows and put aside.

Repeat the entire process with the remaining squares of dough.

The number of ravioli you get and their cooking time depends on how thin you roll your dough. Dump the raviolies into plenty of boiling salted water and cook until the pasta is tender.

## CHEESE FILLING FOR RAVIOLI

This recipe makes enough filling for the Ravioli recipe given above.

>    2 eggs
>    2 cups cottage cheese
>    2 tablespoons fresh parsley
>    dash sea salt
>    ¼ cup grated Parmesan cheese

Break the eggs into your blender container, add the cottage cheese, and blend until smooth. Wash the parsley and cut into 1-inch pieces, add to the egg-cheese mixture, and blend until fine. Blend in the Parmesan and the salt. You may have to help the mixture with your spatula.

## CROQUETTES AND PATTIES

Croquettes and Patties (the same thing, really) are usually fried on top of the stove. This would mean using a great deal of grease and heating it to a very high temperature. Oils heated like that are less useful in making the chains of fatty acids so essential to life. In other words, the grease becomes just fat calories.

Instead, we broil these dishes—that is, cook them *under* the oven's flame (or heating element)—on a lightly vegetable-oiled baking sheet. This uses perhaps a tenth as much grease as top of the stove cooking, and it heats it to a lower temperature. Altogether more desirable.

Unless hand shaping is called for, just drop tablespoonfuls of the batter onto the oiled sheet and put in a cold oven, with the heat at highest setting.

## BUTTERNUT SQUASH CROQUETTES

Butternut is a yellow squash high in vitamin A. It is also very sweet, and available all year round, not just in the fall as with many squashes.

> *1 pound butternut squash*
> *2 eggs*
> *¼ teaspoon sea salt*
> *¼ teaspoon garlic powder*
> *6 tablespoons soy flour*
> *vegetable oil*

Wash and peel the squash (1 pound is about half a medium squash), and cut into ¾-inch chunks. Put into your blender container, cover with water, and blender chop until coarse (see page 9). Drain in a strainer set in a bowl (reserve the water for soup or for baking). Press squash to remove as much water as you can, then scrape the squash into a bowl. Add the eggs, salt, garlic, and soy flour to the bowl and stir well, until uniform. Spoon onto a lightly-oiled baking sheet and put into a cold oven. Set the oven at its highest and broil (that is, under the flame) for 12 to 15

minutes on the first side, then remove from the oven and turn with a pancake turner. Cook on the second side 5 to 7 minutes or until the croquettes begin to brown.
Yield: 12 croquettes.

## CARROT CAKES

The best way to eat carrots is raw, chewed very well. This is just for variety.

> *1 pound carrots*
> *1 large onion*
> *1 teaspoon Dill Salt (see p. 135)*
> *2 eggs*

Wash well, but do not peel, the carrots. Cut into 1-inch chunks and blender chop, covered with water. Pour off into a colander set in a bowl. Peel the onion and cut into chunks. Blender chop, reusing the same water. Pour over the carrots to drain. Press out the water, reserving it for another use, and scrape the mixture into a bowl. Add the Dill Salt and the eggs, and mix well. Spoon heaping table-spoonfuls onto an oiled baking sheet, put into a cold oven, with the heat at its highest setting, and broil for 12 to 15 minutes. Remove, turn gently with a pancake turner, and broil on the second side for about 5 minutes.
Yield: 16 cakes.

## CHICKEN CROQUETTES

We don't have many meat, chicken, or fish recipes in this book, but here's one that's quite different. Tarragon is not an herb that everyone loves at first taste, but if you do like it, you'll love the bit of it in these cakes.
If your family requires more than the 6 cakes this recipe yields, double it without hesitation—but grind the chicken only in ½-cup portions.

½ cup raw chicken meat
1 clove garlic
½ cup nutmeats
½ cup cooked brown rice
¼ teaspoon sea salt
¼ teaspoon dried tarragon
vegetable oil

Trim the skin and fat off one breast and thigh of a 3 pound chicken to get ½ cup of meat. Cut into 1-inch pieces. Grind the chicken by dropping the pieces and the peeled garlic clove through the hole in your blender cap, letting them fall directly on the blades. DO NOT PUT YOUR FINGERS INSIDE THE CONTAINER WITH THE MOTOR ON. Scrape into a bowl.
Coarsely blender chop the nutmeats and add to the chicken and garlic. Measure in the rice, salt, and tarragon and mix well. Spoon onto a lightly oiled baking sheet. Starting in a cold oven, broil at highest heat for about 10 minutes on the first side and 5 to 7 minutes on the second.
Yield: 6 cakes.

## FRUIT CROQUETTES

Here's a most unusual and delicious dish that's perfect for lunch—or for dessert. And that's not a combination you see often. Though there is no sweetener added to the recipe, the fruits are so sweet themselves—and the cooking makes them even sweeter—that you have to eat these croquettes with something sour. We make our own yoghurt, and eat them with that—spooning it right onto the plate and dipping the chunks in. Even the kids will eat yoghurt this way.

2 eggs
8 large dried figs
1 cup pitted dates
1 medium apple
vegetable oil

Break the eggs into the blender. Cut the figs (try to get moist ones) in half and drop a couple of halves at a time through the hole in the blender top, with the motor going at high speed. Scrape out into a bowl. Drop the dates through that same opening, a few at a time (you may have to do it in 2 batches if your blender balks at the full cup) until well blended. Scrape into the same bowl. Wash, core and chunk the apple (don't peel), and, similarly, drop the chunks into the blender a few at a time. Scrape into the bowl, and mix all well. Spoon the mixture onto a lightly oiled baking sheet. Starting in a cold oven, broil at highest temperature for about 7 minutes on the first side and 3 to 4 minutes on the second. Do keep your eyes and nose peeled for this one—the fruit sugars have a tendency to burn if left unwatched.

Yield: 10 cakes.

## PARSNIP PATTIES

Parsnips are rich in potassium and low in sodium, a desirable combination available in many root vegetables. And parsnips prepared like this don't really taste like parsnips (at least to those who dislike parsnips).

> 3 medium, white parsnips
> 1 egg
> ½ teaspoon sea salt
> dash or 2 pepper
> vegetable oil

Wash and trim the parsnips but do not peel them. Cut into ½-inch slices, put in a pot, and cover with *un*salted water. Cook over a medium flame until just soft—about 20 minutes. Remove from the water and lay on a dish or colander to cool until they can be handled. Drop the pieces of parsnip through the hole in the blender top, right onto the blades, with the machine at medium speed. DO NOT PUT YOUR FINGERS INSIDE THE CONTAINER WITH THE MOTOR GOING. You will likely have to grind the parsnips in 2 batches.

Scrape the ground vegetable into a bowl, and add the egg, salt, and pepper. Stir well into a thick mass. Shape into ½-inch patties by hand and place on a lightly oiled baking sheet. Starting in a cold oven and with the temperature set at its highest, broil about 15 minutes on the first side and about 5 minutes on the second side.
Yield: 6 to 8 patties.

## POTATO PANCAKES

Of course, these aren't really pancakes, because pancakes have to be made on the top of the stove (and preferably in a pan); these are much healthier because they aren't fried but broiled. Do use new potatoes when you can get them—they are much less starchy than potatoes that have sat long in the ground or in storage.

> 1¼ pounds new potatoes
> 1 medium onion
> 1 cup bean sprouts
> 2 eggs
> 2 tablespoons soy flour
> 1 teaspoon Sage Salt (see p. 136)
> few dashes pepper
> vegetable oil

Wash and trim (but do not peel) the potatoes. Cut them in half and feed the halves 1 or 2 at a time through the hole in the blender cap. At first they will stay in bits, but when you have enough potato in the blender, it will all liquify, which is what you want. Peel and chunk the onion, add it to the potatoes, and liquify.
Put a couple of thicknesses of cheesecloth in the bottom of a large strainer, set it over a bowl, and pour in the potato and onion mixture. A liquid will drain out through the towel. Let as much drain off as will. When drained, scrape the potato mixture into a bowl, add the sprouts, eggs, soy flour, Sage Salt, and pepper, and mix well. Spoon heaping tablespoons onto a lightly oiled baking sheet and put in a cold broiler with the oven at its highest setting.

Broil for about 12 minutes on the first side, and about 5 minutes on the second side.
Yield: about 20 pancakes, so you will probably have to broil them in 2 batches.

## SOYBURGERS

There are a lot of ingredients in this recipe, but it's really not hard to make.

> *1 medium-small onion*
> *4 tablespoons vegetable oil*
> *2 cups cooked soybeans*
> *1 cup cooked potato*
> *¼ cup fresh bean sprouts*
> *1-1½ teaspoons sea salt*
> *½ teaspoon dried dill weed (see p. 216)*
> *1 teaspoon dried parsley*
> *1 teaspoon dried basil*
> *few dashes of powdered sage*
> *1 teaspoon oregano*
> *vegetable oil*

Peel, chunk, and grind the onions at medium speed. Leave in the container. Add 2 tablespoons vegetable oil and 1 cup soybeans, a tablespoon at a time through the blender cap. Scrape out into a bowl. Grind the rest of the beans with another 2 tablespoons vegetable oil, and scrape out. Dump half the potato into the blender and whirl at low speed until it forms an elastic mass; scrape this mass over the beans. Repeat. (Cooked potato doesn't mash in the blender—it forms this starchy elastic stuff that will help hold the burgers together.) Add the sprouts, salt, and herbs and stir well. If you have the time, let stand for half an hour, to allow the herbs to soak in. Taste for salt. Spoon onto a lightly oiled baking sheet, and broil (starting with a cold oven) at highest heat for 15 minutes on the first side and 5 minutes on the second.
Yield: 10 to 12 large burgers.

## SIMPLE SOYBURGERS

This is a simple recipe compared with the more traditional Soyburger recipe on the previous page.

>*2 cups cooked soybeans*
>*1 pound zucchini*
>*2 eggs*
>*1 tablespoon raw wheat germ*
>*1 cup bean sprouts*
>*vegetable oil*

In 1 or 2 batches grind the soybeans by spooning them through the cap of your blender with the motor going at medium speed (keep your hand over the opening—soybeans tend to fly around). Scrape out into a bowl. Wash and trim but do not peel the zucchini. Cut into 1-inch pieces and grind as you did the beans. Scrape into the same bowl. Add the eggs, wheat germ, and bean sprouts and mix well. Spoon onto a lightly oiled baking sheet. Put in a cold oven set at its highest heat, and broil for about 15 minutes on the first side and about 5 minutes on the second.
Yield: 9 or 10 large burgers.

## SPINACH CROQUETTES

Spinach is a good source of vitamin A and minerals, and available all year round. Also, because it grinds up so readily, it can be used in many kinds of dishes: Noodles, Soufflé, Rabbit, Casserole, etc. This is a well-balanced dish, containing almost every vitamin except a couple of the B's and C (you can't get C in any cooked dish because it's heat sensitive).

>*2 eggs*
>*¼ pound fresh spinach*
>*2 very heaping tablespoons noninstant milk powder*
>*4 tablespoons soy flour*

*3 cups cooked brown rice*
*1 cup fresh bean sprouts*
*vegetable oil*

Break the eggs into the blender. Trim, wash, and drain the spinach (be sure you wash it well—fresh spinach tends to have a lot of sand). Set the blender going at medium speed and feed in the spinach leaves and stalks through the blender top one at a time. DO NOT PUT YOUR FINGERS INTO THE BLENDER CONTAINER WHILE THE MOTOR IS GOING. Blend in the milk powder and soy flour. Scrape into a bowl. Add the rice and the sprouts. Mix well. Spoon onto a lightly oiled baking sheet and broil, starting in a cold oven, with the heat set at its highest, for 15 minutes on the first side and about 5 minutes on the second side. Yield: 12 big, crisp, chewy Croquettes.

## SPINACH-SQUASH CROQUETTES

This is a big recipe, yielding about 24 cakes, so you'll want to broil it in 2 batches.
Zucchini is quite spongy, so, to get the blending water out, pick up handfuls of the chopped squash from the draining colander and *squeeze* until no more water drips out. Repeat this squeezing with subsequent handfuls until all the zucchini is drained and in a mixing bowl. Alternatively, you can do all this draining at once if you have a bowl about the size of your colander: just press the bottom of this bowl against the squash until no more water drips out. Either way, save the water for another use.

*1 pound fresh zucchini*
*2 eggs*
*½ pound spinach*
*½ teaspoon sea salt*
*2 very heaping tablespoons noninstant milk powder*
*⅜ cup whole wheat flour*
*vegetable oil*

Wash and trim, but do not peel, the zucchini; cut into 1-inch chunks, cover with water in the blender, and chop at low speed. Drain as directed above. Break 2 eggs into the blender container. Wash the spinach well and trim off the hard ends. Start the machine going at medium speed and feed the spinach stalks in 1 at a time. DO NOT PUT YOUR FINGERS INSIDE THE CONTAINER WITH THE MOTOR GOING. Increase speed as needed. When blended, add the salt and milk powder and blend again until smooth. Scrape out into the bowl with the zucchini. Add the flour to the other ingredients and mix all together well. Spoon onto a lightly oiled baking sheet. Put into a cold oven set for highest heat and broil for about 12 minutes on the first side and about 5 minutes on the second. For the second batch, because the oven is heated, broil about 7 and 5 minutes. (If the cakes aren't brown, broil longer.) Yield: about 24 croquettes

## FOUR-ROOT PANCAKES

Roots are high in minerals and at their lowest in starch when fresh, that is, newly harvested. Yellow turnips are very nutritious, though not a complete food by any means. You have to watch out, though, their skins are waxed—I suppose for storage purposes. This paraffin coating is not edible, and so the entire skin must be peeled off, unless you get your yellow turnips from a farmer who doesn't wax. What we do is cook up the whole turnip, which is too large for one dish, and have it different ways on different days.

Turnips are best cooked for the blender by peeling, trimming, and then slicing into ½-inch slices, no more than 2 inches across. Put in a pot of unsalted water—to cover—and boil for about 20 minutes. Allow to cool slightly before blending. Cook up more than you need, so you can have turnip for Turnip-Rice Casserole, page 71.

*1 pound raw new potatoes*
*1 large onion*
*½ pound carrots*
*1½ cups cooked yellow turnip chunks*
*2 teaspoons Vegetable Salt (see p. 137)*
*2 eggs*
*2 tablespoons soy flour*
*vegetable oil*

Wash and trim, but do not peel, the potatoes. Cut in half and feed through the opening in your blender top until liquified. Peel the onion, cut in chunks, and add to the potatoes, blending until liquified. Line a large strainer with two thicknesses of cheesecloth and pour in the mixture. Allow to drain until no more liquid drips out. Wash and trim the carrots; cut them into chunks, and blender grind, dropping them onto the blades 1 or 2 at a time, at high speed. Scrape into a bowl. Chop the turnip chunks the same way—in 2 batches. Scrape the ground turnip into the same bowl with the carrots. Add the potato mixture and the salt, eggs, and soy flour. Mix well, Spoon onto a lightly oiled baking sheet, place in a cold oven, and broil at highest heat, about 12 minutes on the first side and 5 minutes on the second.
Yield: about 24 cakes, so broil in 2 batches.

## ZUCCHINI-MUSHROOM CROQUETTES

This is really delicious, but it has a drawback: because of the cheese these croquettes never harden like our others. Our solution has been to broil them on one side only, and then turn them out of the baking sheet very carefully. But it's worth the trouble for this high protein good food.

*2 pounds zucchini*
*½ pound fresh mushrooms*
*½ pound uncolored cheddar cheese*
*1 teaspoon Vegetable Salt (see p. 137)*
*2 eggs*
*vegetable oil*

Wash and trim, but don't peel, the zucchini and cut into 1-inch chunks. Blender chop in 2 parts, covered with water. Set to drain, and squeeze as described on pages 57. If your mushrooms are button-sized, don't cut; if medium cut in half; if large, quarter. Drop, 1 mushroom at a time, through the opening in your blender top, with the motor at lowest speed. Scrape into a bowl. Cut the cheese into ½ to ¾ inch chunks and drop through the opening with the machine going at high speed (keep your hand over the opening—the cheese will fly). Scrape into the same bowl. Add the drained zucchini, Vegetable Salt, and eggs, and mix well. Spoon onto an oiled baking sheet. Start in a cold oven and broil at highest heat, for 12 to 15 minutes ON ONE SIDE ONLY, in 2 batches. Remove carefully.
Yield: about 24 croquettes.

## ZUCCHINI CROQUETTES
It's hard to imagine that something this simple can be this good.

> 1½ pounds zucchini
> 2 rounded tablespoons raw wheat germ
> 3 eggs
> 2 teaspoons Dill Salt (see p. 135)
> vegetable oil

Blender chop the zucchini, covered with water, then drain and squeeze as described on page 57. Scrape into a bowl and add the wheat germ, eggs, and Dill Salt. Mix well. Spoon onto a lightly oiled baking sheet. Starting in a cold oven, broil for 12 to 15 minutes on the first side, and about 5 minutes on the second.
Yield: 12 to 15 croquettes.

# SOUFFLÉS

We hope the word doesn't scare you—there certainly is a kind of snobby mystique around this aspect of French cooking—but Soufflés are easy when you know how.

If you've done the Mousses in the DESSERTS chapter, you know pretty much all about Soufflés, too. These are also made with separated eggs and are intended to be very light and fluffy. But they are baked—and rise in the baking. Don't test Soufflés to see if they are done. We did that on the first we ever tried, and the thing collapsed. The French never test. They look, they smell, they time—but they never test soufflés.

## CHEESE SOUFFLÉ

Here is a dish right out of the heart of French cooking—and yet, with a few changes, it's healthful and nutritious, without the butter and cream called for in French recipes.

> 4 tablespoons vegetable oil
> 1 tablespoon raw wheat germ
> 3 tablespoons whole wheat flour
> 1 cup water
> 1 very heaping tablespoon noninstant milk powder
> ½ teaspoon sea salt
> dash of pepper
> 3-4 ounces uncolored cheddar cheese
> 4 egg yolks
> 4 egg whites

Set the oven to heat to 375°.
Put the first 7 ingredients into the blender and process at low speed until well blended. Pour off into a saucepan and cook over medium heat, stirring, until thick and smooth. Do not boil. When thick, remove from the burner, and allow to cool until you can put a finger in it. Mean-

while, cut the cheese into chunks and grate by dropping through the hole in the blender cover with the blender going at medium speed. When the flour mixture is cooled, add it to the blender and process at medium speed, briefly, until smooth again. Separate the four egg yolks into the blender (put the whites into a bowl for beating), and blend until smooth.

Allow the mixture to cool further, until just warm. Beat the whites until stiff, then fold in the blender mixture quite evenly. Pour carefully into an ungreased 1½ quart casserole. Bake in the preheated oven for 25 minutes, or until the top is brown.

Yield: 4 servings.

## SPINACH SOUFFLÉ

This is a simpler Soufflé—perhaps the easiest we've ever tried.

> 3 tablespoons vegetable oil
> 4 egg yolks
> ¾ cup water
> 1 very heaping tablespoon noninstant milk powder
> 1 tablespoon raw wheat germ
> 1 teaspoon sea salt
> 3 dashes pepper
> ½ pound fresh spinach
> 3 tablespoons whole wheat flour
> 4 egg whites

Set the oven to 375°.

Pour into the blender container: the oil, egg yolks (reserve the whites in a bowl for beating), water, milk powder, wheat germ, salt, and pepper. Blend at low speed until smooth. Wash·and trim the spinach. Feed in through the blender top 1 leaf at a time, increasing speed as needed. DO NOT PUT YOUR FINGERS IN THE CONTAINER WITH THE MOTOR ON. When all the spinach is well blended, blend in the flour. Beat the egg whites until quite stiff. Scrape out the spinach mixture and fold into the whites.

Carefully scrape into an ungreased 1½-quart casserole. Bake in the preheated oven for 30 minutes.
This Soufflé is equally delicious hot or at room temperature.
Yield: 4 servings.

## TURNIP SOUFFLETTE

This is treated as if it were a soufflé so we include it here. It is nowhere near as light as a regular soufflé but it is very tasty, even for those who don't like turnips.

>    2 cups white turnip chunks
>    1 small onion
>    2 tablespoons vegetable oil
>    2 egg yolks
>    ½ teaspoon sea salt
>    2 dashes pepper
>    2 tablespoons honey
>    2 egg whites

Wash and trim, but do not peel, the turnips. Cut into ¾-inch chunks and put into the blender container. Peel and chunk the onion and add to the container. Cover with water and blender chop, then pour into a colander set in a bowl to drain (reserving the water for another use). Oil a skillet, add the drained turnip and onion mixture, and sauté until transparent, about 10 to 15 minutes. When done, remove from the heat and allow to cool somewhat. Put into the blender the egg yolks, salt, pepper, and honey, and blend until smooth. Add the turnip and onion mixture and blend until almost smooth, leaving some bits. Beat the egg whites very stiff. Scrape out the blender mixture and fold it into the whites. Scrape into a greased 1½-quart casserole, put into a cold oven set for 375° to 400°, and bake for about 40 minutes. Serve immediately.
Yield: 4 servings.

## SPINACH NOODLE SOUFFLETTE

Here's another near-soufflé—though the noodles keep it from rising as high. The noodles can be a commercial whole wheat or soy or artichoke kind, or they can be either of the two recipes on pages 47 and 48; cut very thin after rolling.

> 4 egg yolks
> 1 teaspoon sea salt
> 1 teaspoon granulated kelp
> ½ pound fresh spinach
> 1 large scallion
> ½ pound fine noodles, cooked
> 4 egg whites
> 2 tablespoons grated Parmesan cheese

Break the egg yolks into the blender (save the whites in a large bowl), add the salt and kelp. Wash and trim the spinach, then feed in one stalk at a time with the machine at the lowest speed possible. DO NOT PUT YOUR HAND INTO THE CONTAINER WITH THE MOTOR GOING. Wash and trim the scallion, cut into 1-inch pieces, and blend briefly into mixture; you want to taste some scallion bits. Drain the cooked noodles and scrape into a bowl; add the blender mixture and stir well. Beat the egg whites until stiff, then fold into the bowl. Scrape carefully into a greased 2-quart (or larger) casserole. Sprinkle the grated cheese over the top. Starting in a cold oven set at about 400°, bake 30 to 40 minutes.
Yield: 4 servings.

# GRIDDLE CAKES

A griddle is a heavy metal pan with a handle, squarish, usually, and with little or no rim. The thick metal holds the heat and tends to spread it evenly—unlike light aluminum which is hottest right over the heat.

Do not leave your griddle with the grease on for "curing." The griddle should be washed with soap and water after each use, then dried if it is prone to rust.

A griddle is greased only once during each use—before the first batch. If your griddle seems to demand more greasing, throw it out. One of the reasons to own a griddle is to cut down on grease.

The griddle should be well heated before using. A bit of water thrown at the surface should skitter across. Set your flame at high, then reduce it when the griddle is hot enough.

The drawback of griddle cakes is that you can make only about 4 cakes at a time, and so have to stand at the stove, cooking batch after batch. The advantage of griddle cakes is that you can cook stuff much lighter than you can on a baking sheet—and often moister, too.

## BANANA GRIDDLE CAKES

Make this recipe with ripe bananas—the ones that have already begun to turn brown.

        3 eggs
        1 tablespoon honey
        ½ cup water
        1 pound bananas (weighed before peeling)
        ½ cup whole wheat flour
        ½ cup raisins
        vegetable oil

Break the eggs into the blender container and add the honey and water. Blend briefly. Peel and break up the bananas. Add to container and blend until smooth. Blend

in the flour, then process the raisins briefly—you want raisin bits. Grease and heat the griddle until water skitters over it. From the blender pour out batter into the quadrants of the griddle. You want cakes that are 3 to 4 inches across. Cook until brown on the first side, then turn with a pancake turner to cook on the other side. Time depends on the heat of your griddle. Repeat until all the batter is cooked. This is a truly memorable breakfast.
Yield: about 24 cakes.

## BLUEBERRY TAN CAKES

These are *Tan* Cakes because they are made with both whole wheat and unbleached white flour. This makes a lot of cakes, but any leftovers will keep in the refrigerator for a week.

> 4 eggs
> 1 cup water
> 1 tablespoon honey
> 1 cup blueberries
> 1 cup whole wheat flour
> ½ cup unbleached white flour
> vegetable oil

Break the eggs into the blender, add the water and honey, and blend until smooth. Wash the berries in hot water, stem, and blend very briefly. Add the flours, stir in with your spatula, and blend at lowest possible speed until all the flour is wet. Preheat and grease the griddle, then pour small amounts of batter onto the 4 quadrants. Turn when brown on the first side.
Yield: about 30 cakes.

## BUCKWHEAT GRIDDLE CAKES

Buckwheat is a distinctive and unusual flavor—one the kids may not go for at once. This is not a big recipe, enough for a big Sunday brunch for 2.

3 eggs
1 tablespoon honey
½ cup water
1 apple
¾ cup buckwheat flour
vegetable oil

Break the eggs into the blender container and add the honey and water. Wash and core, but do not peel, the apple, and cut it into chunks. Drop into the blender container and process at medium speed until smooth. Add the buckwheat flour and blend again until smooth. Preheat and grease your griddle, then pour small amounts of batter into the 4 quadrants. Turn when slightly brown on the first side. Yield: 16 cakes.

## CHEESE GRIDDLE CAKES

Here's a recipe that's different, but one everyone will love —everyone who likes cheese, that is. These cakes come out thicker than the other Griddle Cake recipes—some as much as ⅜ inch—which means slightly longer cooking time.

3 eggs
¾ cup water
1 cup whole wheat flour
¼ pound cheese
vegetable oil

Break the eggs into the blender container and add the water. Measure in the flour and blend until uniform. Cut the cheese into ½-inch chunks and feed through the blender top a few at a time, until all is smooth. Preheat and grease your griddle, then pour on the batter, making 4 cakes at a time. Turn when lightly brown on the first side. Yield: about 16 cakes.

## COTTAGE CHEESE GRIDDLE CAKES

These cakes are naturally moist, and you'll probably want to keep them moist by cooking just a bit less than our other Griddle Cakes.

> 3 eggs
> ¾ cup water
> 1 apple
> ½ cup whole wheat flour
> 1 cup (½ pound) cottage cheese
> vegetable oil

Break the eggs into the blender container and add the water. Wash and core, but do not peel, the apple. Cut into chunks and drop 1 chunk at a time through the opening in the blender cover, with the motor at medium speed. Blend in the flour. Add the cottage cheese, mix in with your spatula, then blend briefly, just to distribute the cottage cheese. Grease and preheat your griddle, then pour batter onto the 4 quarters of the griddle. Turn when the first side begins to brown. To keep the cakes moist, keep the heat high; to let them dry a bit more, cook over medium-low heat.
Yield: about 24 cakes.

## SPINACH-CHEESE GRIDDLE CAKES

You don't think spinach makes a breakfast? Try these and see.

> 3 eggs
> ½ cup water
> ¼ pound spinach
> ¼ pound uncolored cheddar cheese
> ½ cup whole wheat flour
> vegetable oil

Break the eggs into the blender and add the water. Wash and trim the spinach; drain but don't dry it (the water left

on the drained spinach is figured into the recipe). With the blender starting at lowest speed, feed the stalks in one at a time until all are blended. DO NOT PUT YOUR FINGERS IN THE CONTAINER WHILE THE MOTOR IS RUNNING. Cut the cheese into 1-inch cubes, and drop into the mixture, a few cubes at a time, with the motor at medium speed. When smooth, blend in the flour. Grease and preheat your griddle, then pour the batter into the 4 quadrants. Turn when brown on first side. These will come out very thin and crisp if you give them the chance.
Yield: more than 2 dozen cakes.

# CASSEROLES

These simple dishes provide main courses for at least 4 hearty eaters, or side vegetables for a large dinner party.

## CABBAGE CASSEROLE

Cabbage is cheap and readily available, and the eggs and soybeans make for a goodly amount of complete protein in this very tasty dish.

> 2 pounds cabbage
> 2 cups cooked soybeans
> 1 cup nutmeats
> 2 teaspoons sea salt
> 1 cup raisins
> 5 egg yolks
> ¼ cup honey
> 5 egg whites

Wash and trim the cabbage and cut into wedges. Further cut the wedges into chunks and blender chop in 2 or 3 batches, covered with water; drain (reserving the water for another use). Grind the soybeans by spooning through the opening in the blender top, with the motor at medium speed. Scrape into a large bowl. Coarsely chop the nutmeats at low speed. Scrape into the bowl. Add the drained cabbage, salt, whole raisins, egg yolks, and honey. Mix very well. Beat the egg whites in a bowl until stiff; fold them into the cabbage mixture. Scrape into an ungreased large casserole, set in a cold oven, and bake for about 40 minutes at about 400°.

Yield: 4 servings.

## CARROT-RICE CASSEROLE

For a little more bite, uncolored sharp cheddar cheese can be substituted for the Swiss.

> 2 cups carrot chunks
> 1 large onion
> 3 eggs
> 1 teaspoon sea salt
> 1 teaspoon thyme
> ½ pound Swiss cheese
> 2 cups cooked brown rice
> 1 cup fresh bean sprouts

Wash and trim, but do not peel, the carrots. Cut into 1-inch pieces and blender chop, covered with water. Drain and reuse the water for the onion. Trim the onion, chunk, and blender chop. Drain, reserving the water for another use. Break the eggs into the blender. Add the salt and thyme. Cut the cheese into ¾-inch cubes, and drop them a few at a time through the opening in the blender top, with the motor at high speed. Scrape the mixture into a large bowl. Scrape in the cabbage and onion, add the rice and bean sprouts, and mix well. Dump into a 1½ quart casserole and bake in a medium oven for 45 minutes, (pre-

heating is not necessary) then set the heat at high temperature for 5 minutes before removing from the oven to crisp the top.
Yield: 4 servings.

## TURNIP-RICE CASSEROLE

> 2 cups cooked yellow turnip chunks
> 1 medium onion
> 3 eggs
> ¼ cup milk or skim milk
> 6 ounces uncolored cheddar cheese
> 1 teaspoon sea salt
> dash or 2 pepper
> 2 cups cooked brown rice
> 1 cup fresh bean sprouts

Cook the turnips according to directions on page 58, and blender grind by dropping a chunk at a time through the opening in your blender top, with the blender going at medium speed. Scrape into a large bowl. Peel the onion and cut into chunks, then process the same way, and scrape into the bowl. Break the eggs into the blender container and add the milk. Cut the cheese into ¾-inch chunks and process by dropping a few at a time through that opening with the motor going at medium speed. When smooth, scrape into the bowl with the turnip and onion mixture and add the rest of the ingredients. Mix well and, starting in a cold oven, bake in an ungreased 1½-quart casserole at medium heat for about 45 minutes.
Yield: 4 large servings.

## ZUCCHINI CASSEROLE

This dish comes out a little wetter than the other Casseroles because cottage cheese tends to express liquid when cooked, while eggs tend to bind up a recipe. But the crisp zucchini and chewy rice come out tasting so good that it's worth being unconventional.

> 2 pounds fresh zucchini
> 1 medium onion
> 2 cups cottage cheese
> 2 cups cooked brown rice
> 1 teaspoon sea salt
> 1 teaspoon dried dill weed (see p. 216)

Wash and trim, but do not peel, the zucchini. Cut into ½-inch pieces and blender chop, covered with water. Drain in a colander set in a bowl. Reuse the water to blender chop the peeled onion. Pour the chopped onion over the squash. Press out the liquid as described on page 57, then scrape the mixture into a large bowl. (Reserve the water for soup or some other use.) Into the bowl, add the cottage cheese, rice, salt, and dill weed, and mix well.
Bake in an ungreased 2-quart casserole for only 25 to 30 minutes at high temperature. Keep your nose peeled for scorching if your oven tends to get very hot very fast.
Yield: 4 hearty servings.

# RABBITS

Of course, there is no meat in these Rabbits—it's a joke: "Welsh Rabbit." New Englanders serve codfish as "Cape Cod Turkey." And according to the best information we can find, the use of the word "Rarebit" is the result of humorless people trying to make sense out of the joke.
So, what you get is a meatless dish, but a dish that has a good deal of animal protein in the forms of egg and cheese.
The traditional way of serving Rabbits is to spoon them over slices of bread, but we recommend that you serve them over brown rice or the whole grain Noodles on pages 47 and 48.
These are not large recipes. We find that for dinner they will feed 4, but that's stretching a little.

## GREEN RABBIT

Here's another way to serve spinach, either for lunch or dinner. If the green color doesn't bother you, it's really delicious.

> 3 eggs
> ½ pound fresh spinach
> ½ teaspoon sea salt
> ½ pound uncolored cheddar cheese
> 1 tablespoon soy flour

Break the eggs into your blender container. Wash and trim the hard bottoms off the spinach and drain well, patting dry gently with a clean towel. Feed the spinach stalks 1 at a time through the opening in your blender top, increasing the speed when the machine balks. DO NOT PUT YOUR FINGERS INTO THE CONTAINER WHILE THE MOTOR IS GOING. When the spinach is all blended, add the salt. Cut the cheese into ¾-inch chunks, and also feed through the top of the blender, with the motor at medium speed, until smooth. Blend in the soy flour. Scrape the whole mixture (it will look grainy from the cheese) into a large saucepan and turn the heat to medium. Cook, stirring, until the mixture thickens—only a few minutes.
Serve immediately over hot brown rice or noodles.
Yield: 4 servings.

## RED RABBIT

This is a dish in which the tomato taste really comes to the fore—you can't taste the higher calcium content.

> ½ pound ripe tomatoes
> 1 very heaping tablespoon noninstant milk powder
> dash mustard powder
> 2 eggs
> ½ pound uncolored cheddar cheese
> 1 tablespoon whole wheat flour

Wash and trim the tomatoes and cut into quarters. Blend at high speed until liquified. Add the milk powder, mustard, and eggs, and blend briefly. Cut the cheddar into ¾-inch chunks and feed into the mixture a few at a time with the blender going at medium speed. When smooth, blend in the flour. Turn the mixture into a saucepan and cook over medium heat, stirring, until it thickens.
Serve immediately over hot brown rice or noodles.
Yield: 4 servings.

# LOAVES

These meat loaves (and *no*-meat loaf) are economical and very tasty, but they are work. They must be prepared, and blended, and then baked. But comes the cold weather, Soups and Loaves make very satisfying meals, at pennies per serving.

## VEAL KIDNEY LOAF

In most supermarkets you can find beef and veal kidneys quite easily. Lamb kidney, which used to be a favorite of ours, has increased by 50 percent in price, and pork kidney is, after all, pork—which we avoid. So we make this very tasty loaf with veal kidney, as it is a bit milder than the beef.
Veal and beef kidney come with a large chunk of fat right in the middle. To prepare the kidney for cooking, wash (you may have to peel off a tough outer membrane if the butcher has not), and then trim the kidney away from the fat with a sharp knife. You don't mind cutting the kidney up this way because you want chunks small enough for the skillet.
If you don't have dried corn kernels, substitute about ¼ cup yellow corn meal. If you must buy corn meal, buy only meal that is *not* degerminated. Corn meal with the germ removed is missing important nutritional values.

½ cup dried corn kernels
½ cup dried lentils
1½ cups warm water
1 tablespoon wine
1 medium veal kidney (about ¾ pound)
1 large onion
2 tablespoons wine (additional)
1 egg
½ teaspoon dried basil (see p. 216)
½ teaspoon leaf sage
¼ teaspoon fennel seed
½ teaspoon Dill Salt (see p. 135)
3 dashes pepper

Blender grind the corn and lentils to a fine meal as directed on page 217. Scrape out of the blender and into a bowl. Add the water and 1 tablespoon of wine and stir. Allow to sit for about 30 minutes.

Wash and trim the kidney and put the pieces into a large skillet. Peel and chunk the onion and add to the skillet. Set for medium heat and sauté for about 5 minutes, turning the kidney and stirring the onion as needed. (You'll notice we haven't used any oil —the kidney supplies its own grease.) When the kidney looks brown all over, remove from the heat and allow to cool for a few minutes. Spoon the kidney and onion into the blender (don't wash the skillet) and add 2 tablespoons wine, the egg, basil, sage, fennel, salt, and pepper. Blend at low speed until coarsely chopped.

Add the wet corn-lentil mixture to the skillet and, over low heat, bring to a simmer and stir until a thickish mush. Add the blender mixture to this, and stir well, with the flame off.

Scrape into an ungreased 8-inch baking pan and put into a cold oven. Bake for 10 minutes at highest setting, and then reduce the heat to medium and bake for another 35 minutes.

This will not slice well, so just spoon out of the pan.

Yield: 4 servings.

## STRETCH MEAT LOAF

Adelle Davis is of the opinion that organ meats help de-
velop the same organ in man: that is, hearts to strengthen
our hearts; brains to make the kids smarter. We don't
know, but we do know that organ meats are full of good
nutritional values, and often they are the cheapest meats in
your butcher's meat case. Here's a way to feed about 6
people for about 70¢ worth of meat.

> 1 cup dried corn
> 1 cup dried soybeans
> 3 cups water
> 1 pound calf heart
> 1 pound onion
> 1 egg
> 2 teaspoons Onion Salt (see p. 138)
> 1 teaspoon dried basil (see p. 216)
> 1 teaspoon thyme
> 3 dashes pepper

Blender grind the corn berries as described on page 217,
and reserve in a bowl. Repeat with the soybeans, and add
to the same bowl. Add 3 cups water and stir, allowing to
stand for about 30 minutes.
Wash the heart and trim off any fat and visible arteries.
Slice into ½-inch strips and lay in a large ungreased skillet.
Peel and hand chop the onions coarsely, and add to the
skillet. Sauté over medium heat until the heart looks just
brown on both sides—about 5 minutes. Stir and turn as
needed.
When the heart looks brown (the onion will be barely
transparent) remove from the heat and allow to cool for
5 minutes. Reserve the onions on a dish and fork the heart
slices into the blender. Add the egg, salt, basil, thyme, and
pepper, and blend at low speed until coarsely chopped.
You'll probably have to shut the blender off several times
to help the mixture onto the blades with your rubber
spatula.
Pour the corn and soybean stuff into the skillet and, over
low heat, bring to a simmer, stirring until a thick mush

(only a minute or so). When thick, shut off the heat, add the onions, add the blender mixture, stir well, and scrape into 2 ungreased 7½-inch baking pans.
Bake for 10 minutes at highest heat, and then for an additional 25 minutes at medium.
Yield: 6 servings.

## CHICK LOAF

This dish is very like a meat loaf in texture, but a bit drier. Serve it with one of the Ketchups in Chapter 3 and it's a treat. Because the chick-peas have to soak overnight, this recipe requires some planning.

> ½ pound chick-peas, soaked
> ½ pound onion
> 1 clove garlic
> 2 teaspoons dried basil (see p. 216)
> ½ teaspoon ground fennel (see p. 216)
> ¾ teaspoon sea salt
> dash pepper
> 2 teaspoons vegetable oil
> 1 egg
> additional vegetable oil

The night before, soak chick-peas in enough water to cover twice.
Next day, grind the chick-peas by spooning them through the opening in the top of your blender with the machine going at medium speed. You may need 2 batches to grind them all. Scrape into a bowl. Peel and chunk the onion; peel the garlic. Drop through the blender top and chop at medium speed. Scrape into the bowl. Add the basil, fennel, salt, pepper, 2 teaspoons oil, and egg and mix well. Lightly grease a 7-inch loaf pan with vegetable oil, spoon the mixture in, and bake about 35 minutes in a 350 to 400 degree oven.

# MISCELLANY

## WHEAT GERM CREPES

Crepes make a lovely main course, and one that really brings looks of amazement to the faces of family and friends. And so long as you use wholesome ingredients there is no real health drawback to serving them. The oil used in cooking them does get heated pretty hot, but we use very little—less than 2 tablespoons for the whole recipe.

Unfortunately, you have to cook Crepes 1 at a time. You have to stand (or sit on a stool) at the oven and drip the oil into the pan, pour and swirl the batter turn the Crepe, dump it from the pan, and repeat, 10 to 12 times for the whole batch. But Crepes are good and they are impressive. The recipe for Blintzes filling on pages 79–80 goes well with this recipe. But you can use any filling you like. Try the Chicken Pâté on page 118; or the Fish Spread on page 119. Or even just wrap the Crepes around pieces of cooked chicken or fish.

> 4 eggs
> 1 cup water
> 1 tablespoon honey
> 1 apple
> 1 very heaping tablespoon noninstant milk powder
> 1/3 cup raw wheat germ
> 2/3 cup unbleached white flour
> vegetable oil

Break the eggs into the blender container and add the water and honey. Wash and core, but do not peel, the apple; cut into chunks and drop a few at a time through the opening in the blender top, with the blender at high speed until liquified. Add the milk powder, wheat germ, and flour, and blend for about 30 seconds at medium speed.

To cook Crepes: Use a light frying pan about 7 inches across the bottom (a smaller pan will just make more Crepes; a larger pan will be difficult to handle). It is not necessary to use a special crepes pan—we have found them heavy to the wrist and no better in the final Crepes. Turn your burner on high. Pour about 1 tablespoon of oil into the bottom of the pan, swish it around, then pour off all the oil that will pour (into a small cup, say). Allow to get quite hot, then reduce the heat. Scoop out a 2 tablespoon measure of batter and pour it into the pan with a circular motion—to spread it over as much of the pan as possible. As you pour tilt the pan back and forth until the batter is spread as thin and even as it will get. Cook until the bottom begins to brown (you are allowed to peek—just lift the corner with a spatula), then turn the Crepe onto its other side. You can turn Crepes without a spatula. Tilt the pan and shake it to loosen the Crepe (you may have to shake quite vigorously), then lift the Crepe by the far edge and pull it toward you as you lift. Or you can slip your spatula under the Crepe and just turn it. Cook briefly on the other side, then turn out onto a plate. Add a few drops of oil to the pan after every 2 Crepes.

When all are cooked, either fill with a filling and reheat under the broiler, or allow to cool and use a cold filling. Yield: about 10 Crepes.

## BLINTZES

This recipe calls for 1 egg yolk. You can include the egg white in the Crepes recipe, rather than keep it lying around in the refrigerator.

Maple syrup is the condensed sap of sugar maple trees. Most of the "maple" syrups in your supermarket have never been *close* to a maple tree. They are "maple flavored," and even those that do contain some real maple syrup have no more than a few percent—the other 97% is sugar and chemicals and water. If you can't get *real* maple syrup, substitute honey.

> 10 cooked Crepes (see preceding recipe)
> 1/4 lemon rind
> 1 egg yolk
> 1 tablespoon maple syrup
> 1 cup cottage cheese
> vegetable oil

Grind the lemon peel with the blender going at high speed (shut the machine off once or twice and scrape the bits down to the bottom). Add the egg yolk and the maple syrup, and blend briefly. Add the cottage cheese, and with your scraper mix it well (while in the blender). Blend very briefly, then scrape out into a bowl.

Spoon 1 rounded tablespoon of filling into the center of a Crepe, and fold the Crepe like an envelope: the bottom over, then the sides in, then the top over. Place on a lightly oiled baking sheet as rolled. Broil under medium-high heat for about 10 minutes.

Yield: 10 Blintzes.

## VEAL AND PEPPERS

Here's a delicious combination that takes very little time to prepare. If you can't afford veal, substitute chicken. And make sure your green peppers aren't waxed.

> vegetable oil
> 1 pound onions
> 4 small cloves garlic
> 1 1/2 large green bell peppers
> 3/4 pound boneless veal shoulder
> 2 tablespoons tamari soy sauce
> 1/2 cup wine

Oil a quite large skillet. Peel the onions and garlic and coarsely hand chop. Put into the skillet. Wash the pepper, cut coarsely, and put into the skillet. Sauté at medium-high heat until the onions brown.

Meanwhile, wash and trim any fat from the veal. Cut into ¾-inch bits. Dump half the bits into the blender and cover with water. Blender chop at low speed for about 20 seconds (you want a texture like finely chopped hamburger). Be sure you have your blender top on securely and that you hold onto the machine while blending—your machine will resent having to process raw meat, but can do it. When blended, allow to drain in a strainer set in a bowl, and reuse the water to process the second batch of meat. Allow to drain but do not force water out of the draining meat—some of that water will help to make our gravy. Any leftover water makes a happy addition to a soup.

Add the tamari and wine to the cooked vegetables (with the heat still on) and stir. Add the meat and stir well, distributing through the dish. Cover and cook for only 3 minutes more.

Serve over hot brown rice.

Yield: 4 large helpings.

## LEFTOVER DINNER

Here's a winner, about the consistency of "Sloppy Joes" but nutritionally excellent.

Any leftover meat (or poultry) will do. We hope that you don't cook the enzymes out of all your meat—well-done meat is a second-rate food. Also, well-done meat will have little flavor after reheating.

If you don't have any leftover meat, you can start with raw —just cut about ½ pound raw lean meat into ¼ to ½-inch pieces, place in the skillet, and, without any additional grease, sauté until just done, stirring occasionally.

If you have no leftover rice (how flexible can you get!), use the tomato and meat mixture as a tomato sauce for Pasta.

1½ pounds tomatoes
2 tablespoons wine
3 tablespoons tamari soy sauce
1 teaspoon oregano
1 tablespoon basil (see p. 216)
½ teaspoon dill seed
½ teaspoon fennel seed
1 rounded tablespoon granulated kelp
2 large cloves garlic
1 small onion
1 medium green pepper
¾-1 cup leftover meat
2-3 cups leftover brown rice

Wash and quarter the tomatoes, dump all into the blender, and process at highest speed until liquified. Add the wine, tamari, oregano, basil, dill and fennel seeds, and kelp, and blend in at low speed. Peel the garlic, peel and quarter the onion, and add both to the blender. Blend at medium speed until well processed. Seed the pepper, wash it well, and chunk it. Blend at medium speed briefly until in small bits, but not all gone.

Pour this tomato mixture into a large, ungreased, skillet. Cut the meat into ½-inch strips and dump in, along with the cold rice. Stir all well, and heat over medium flame until the mixture is hot enough to serve—no more than 5 minutes.

Yield: 4 servings.

## STUFFED CABBAGE

This dish is delicious and much easier than your grand-mother told you. Have toothpicks on hand to hold the cabbage rolls together. Some small care is required in bending the large cabbage leaves without breaking them through. (Most recipes call for precooking the leaves to soften them, but this way they come out crisper.) Remember, it doesn't matter if you crack the spine of a leaf, so long as it still will hold the stuffing.

If you have no Vegetable Stock, here's a chance to use all that blender water you've been saving "for another use."

> 2 cups cooked soybeans
> 2 eggs
> 1 medium onion
> 2 cups cooked brown rice
> 1 cup raisins
> dash sea salt
> dash pepper
> 8 large cabbage leaves
> Vegetable Stock (see p. 18)

At medium speed grind the soybeans by spooning a tablespoon at a time through the opening in your blender top. You will likely need to grind them in 2 batches. Scrape into a bowl. Break the eggs into the blender. Peel the onion, chunk it, and chop it briefly in the eggs at low speed. Scrape into the bowl. Add the rice and raisins, and taste for the addition of salt or pepper. Peel 8 large, green outside leaves from a head of cabbage and wash them well. Spoon an eighth of the mixture onto a leaf, fold the top and bottom over, and then fold the sides in. Fasten the sides down with a toothpick on each side, and place on edge in a pot large enough to hold the entire recipe. Repeat with the rest of the leaves and stuffing, standing each stuffed leaf on its edge in the pot. Cover with Vegetable Stock, or blender water if you have no stock. Bring to the boil and simmer for 20 minutes, uncovered.
The stock is enriched from this use and makes an even better soup to go with the cabbage.
Yield: 4 servings.

# DRESSINGS,
# SALADS,
# AND SAUCES

This is a mixed bag of a chapter, containing topics as diverse as Pickles and Mayonnaise.

Most sauces, in the traditional French or Italian styles, must be simmered for hours to get out the delicate flavors (or that's what people who simmer things for hours tell us). With a blender, all that simmering is forgotten, and you can have a tomato sauce even on a hot summer day, and a tomato sauce with its nutrition intact.

If your digestive tract argues with you about the mustard in some of these Dressing recipes, drop it. These Dressings don't depend on the mustard.

# MAYONNAISES

The main reason we make rather than buy mayonnaise is that mayonnaise is a Standard of Identity food, which means that the maker is not required to list his ingredients on the label. Hellmann's may advertise that the whole egg goes into Hellmann's, but we have no idea of what else goes in, except for very broad labeling. There are egg substitutes and other substitutions that do not have to be listed on the label.

If you wish, you can get a copy of the Standard of Identity for Salad Dressings (which includes mayonnaise) by requesting it from the nearest branch of the Department of Health, Education, and Welfare. They will also send you on request a list of the dozens of foods that fall under Standard of Identity regulations, including bread, cheese, chocolate, and soft drinks. One source has it that about 20 percent of the food eaten in the United States falls under the Standard of Identity regulations.

There are exceptions. Special diet foods are required to list their ingredients—so you may see a diet or low-calorie mayonnaise with its ingredients listed.

By the way, you can make a tasy mayonnaise without a blender—but it can never have that marvelous thick texture.

## BASIC MAYONNAISE

This recipe, other than the addition of a little wheat germ, is traditional. (See the next recipe for an explanation of cold-pressed oils.)

> 1 egg
> ½ teaspoon dry English mustard
> ½ teaspoon sea salt
> 1 teaspoon raw wheat germ
> 3 tablespoons cider vinegar
> 1 cup cold-pressed vegetable oil

Break the egg into your blender container and add the mustard, salt, wheat germ, and vinegar. Blend until smooth at low speed. With the machine going at low speed, drip in, through the hole in the blender top, ¼ cup or less of oil. Blend for about 30 seconds, then slowly dribble in another ¼ cup or less. Blend until the mixture begins to thicken—as much as 1 minute. Dribble in another ¼ cup, blending until thick. Stop the blender and pour in the remaining oil, and stir in with your spatula. Blend the mixture until smooth. The resulting Mayonnaise will be too thick to pour, so scrape it into a jar for storage in the refrigerator, or into a bowl for serving.

This will not keep for months, as does commercial mayonnaise. It contains no preservatives, and the egg will go bad after about a month in the refrigerator. But certainly, a month is long enough to keep any food.

Yield: almost 1½ cups.

## HERBED MAYONNAISE

The flavor of this mayonnaise is an eye opener.

All our mayonnaise recipes call for cold-pressed oil. Oils are necessary in building the fatty acids, essential to life; cold pressed oils are the most nutritious you can find. Most commercial oils are extracted from the corn kernel or cottonseed or soybean, or whatever, by a solvent process. This solvent is never completely removed from the oil. So, if you eat supermarket oil you are probably eating solvent, too. Other oils (called cold pressed, although they really are not) are pressed from the kernels in a process that generates heat, which destroys the vitamin E but leaves no solvent. The oils pressed this way look much like the solvent oils. Then there is a group of oils that is really cold pressed. They are more expensive than the commercial oils, but they have vitamin E *and* no solvent. The Erewhon Company in Boston, for example, is a producer of several truly cold-pressed oils: they look much darker than supermarket oils and they have some of the sediment still in the bottle.

1 egg
½ teaspoon dry English mustard
½ teaspoon raw wheat germ
1 teaspoon ground marjoram
¼ teaspoon leaf thyme
3 tablespoons wine vinegar
1 cup cold pressed oil

Break the egg into the blender container and add the rest of the ingredients, except the oil. Blend until smooth at low speed. Add about ¼ cup oil and blend for almost 1 minute at low speed. With the machine still at low, dribble in another ¼ cup or less of oil and blend until thickened. Blend in the remaining oil ¼ cup at a time.
Yield: almost 1½ cups.

## CHEESE MAYONNAISE

The flavor of Cheese Mayonnaise varies, of course, with the flavor of the cheese: for a sharp Mayonnaise, use a sharp cheddar cheese; for a milder Mayonnaise, use a mild cheddar or a Muenster.

2 small lemons
1 egg
½ teaspoon dry mustard
¼ pound cheese
¾ cup cold-pressed oil

Wash, peel, and pit the lemons; put the pulp in the blender and liquify at highest speed. Add the egg and the mustard and blend briefly. Cut the cheese into ½-inch cubes and blend at low speed 1 or 2 at a time until the mixture is quite smooth. With the motor still on low, dribble in ¼ cup oil or less. Blend for about 30 seconds. Add another ¼ cup, and blend until the mixture thickens—about 1 minute. Blend in the rest of the oil for a few seconds.
Yield: about 1½ cups.

## DILL-ONION MAYONNAISE

We use dried dill weed in this recipe because it's easier to handle than the fresh in this small amount.

> 1 egg
> 2 teaspoons onion bits
> 1 teaspoon dried dill weed (see p. 216)
> ½ teaspoon Dill Salt (see p. 135)
> ¼ teaspoon dry mustard
> ½ cup cold pressed vegetable oil

Break the egg into the blender. Add the onion, dill weed, Dill Salt, and mustard. Blend until smooth. With the motor at low speed, drip in a small amount of the oil, and allow to blend for about 15 seconds. Dribble in some more oil until you have ¼ cup total in the blender. Blend for about 30 seconds. Dribble in another fraction and blend until the mixture thickens. Blend in the remaining oil. Yield: almost 1 cup.

## GARLIC MAYONNAISE

This has a definite, but not a strong, garlic flavor. It would be equally good on salad or cold fish, or as an artichoke dip.

> 1 egg
> 2½ tablespoons wine vinegar
> 1 large clove garlic
> ½ teaspoon dry mustard
> ½ teaspoon sea salt
> 1 teaspoon raw wheat germ
> 1 cup cold-pressed vegetable oil

Break the egg into the blender. Add the vinegar and blend until smooth. Peel and halve the garlic, and add it along with the mustard, salt, and wheat germ. Blend until smooth.

With the motor on low speed, dribble in about ¼ cup oil. Blend for about 30 seconds. Dribble in a second ¼ cup and blend for about 1 minute. Add a third ¼ cup and blend until thick. Blend in the last of the oil.
Yield: almost 1½ cups.

## GREEN MAYONNAISE

Because of the water *in* the vegetables (not *on* them) this Mayonnaise comes out thinner than most of the others, but it's still a Mayonnaise for all that. Also, the raw green vegetables give it a small nutritional bonus.

> *1 lemon*
> *1 egg*
> *2 teaspoons raw wheat germ*
> *½ teapsoon mustard*
> *¼ teaspoon sea salt*
> *6 sprigs watercress*
> *2 ounces fresh spinach*
> *1 cup cold-pressed oil*

Wash, peel, and seed the lemon, then liquify at high speed. Add the egg, wheat germ, mustard, and salt, and blend at low speed until smooth. Wash the watercress and the spinach (leaves and stems) well, and pat dry with a towel. With the blender on low, feed in the watercress, then the spinach 1 stalk at a time, increasing the speed if necessary. When the greens are all blended in, dribble in ¼ cup oil with the motor going at the lowest speed possible. Blend for about 30 seconds. Add a second ¼ cup oil, blend again for 30 seconds. Dribble in the remaining oil, allowing some blending between dribbles. Do not expect this to thicken like the other Mayonnaises.
Yield: almost 2 cups.

## LIME-MINT MAYONNAISE

This eggless recipe is for those who like a strongly tart salad dressing. For a less tart Mayonnaise, use only one lime. This, too, comes out rather thin.

> 2 small limes
> 1 teaspoon dried mint
> 1 teaspoon onion bits (or 1 scallion top)
> ½ teaspoon sea salt
> ½ teaspoon dry mustard
> ¾ cup cold-pressed oil

Wash, peel, and pit the limes, then liquify at high speed. Add the mint, the onion, salt, and mustard, and blend at low speed until smooth. Dribble in ¼ cup oil with the motor on low speed and blend for 30 seconds. Add the remaining oil, ¼ cup at a time, allowing about 30 seconds of blending between dribbles.
Yield: about 1 cup.

## SAUCE NIÇOISE

When you see a recipe name including "Niçoise" you can be fairly certain that tomatoes enter into it somewhere.
Though this is called a sauce, it is actually a salad dressing or cold meat or fish dressing. Don't pour it on pasta—unless it's cold pasta.
Onion sprouts are what you get when you leave an onion around too long.

> ¼ pound tomatoes
> ½ green pepper
> 1 or 2 sprigs scallion tops or onion sprouts
> 1 cup Mayonnaise

Use any of our Mayonnaises except Lime-Mint Mayonnaise
—its flavor is too strong for this sauce.
Wash and quarter the tomatoes and put in the blender.
Wash and chunk the pepper, and add to blender. Wash
and cut up the onion sprouts or scallions, and blend all
at high speed until liquid. Pour from the blender into a
strainer and allow to drain (save the drained liquid—it's
delicious). When drained, mix the vegetables with the
Mayonnaise by hand.
Yield: 1½ cups.

# SALAD DRESSINGS

Salad Dressings whip up in little time in the blender, and
for the most part they don't separate (if they do, a quick
shake puts them together again). The blender allows you
to use fresh lemon instead of bottled reconstituted lemon
juice. It allows you to blend garlic right into the dressing.
It allows you to make fresh chopped herbs an integral
part of the dressing. The blender even allows you to make
the far-out Nut Dressing on page 94.

## BASIC FRENCH DRESSING

The French generally don't include the garlic in the finished
dressing but like the Chinese, they pull it out before serving. We like to keep the garlic—in both Fernch and
Chinese cooking.

>    1 clove garlic
>    1/3 cup mild cider vinegar
>    1 tablespoon raw wheat germ
>    1 teaspoon sea salt
>    1 cup cold-pressed oil

Peel the garlic clove and quarter it. Put it in the blender container with the rest of the ingredients and blend until smooth.
Yield: 1¼ cups.

## HERB DRESSING

Perhaps lecithin should be an ingredient in all oil dressings. Its constituents are two B vitamins, choline and inositol (from soybeans), and it helps the system dissolve cholesterol. Commercially it is used as an emulsifier.
Notice that this recipe calls for *fresh* dill weed and parsley, not dried.

> 2 *lemons*
> 1 *clove garlic*
> 1 *tablespoon raw wheat germ*
> 1 *tablespoon lecithin granules*
> 1 *teaspoon sea salt*
> 1 *cup cold-pressed oil*
> 1 *ounce combined fresh dill weed and parsley*

Wash, peel, and pit the lemons, then liquify at high speed. Peel and halve the garlic and add it to the blender with the wheat germ, lecithin, salt, and oil. Blend until smooth. Wash the herbs well and pat half dry in a towel. Cut into 1-inch pieces and blend with the other ingredients until well chopped.
Yield: 1½ cups.

## LEMON DRESSING

Because it contains less oil, this dressing tastes more lemony than the Herb Dressing.
Potassium chloride is a salt substitute—one that brings you a little potassium to balance the salt (sodium) that may be

too abundant in your diet. Almost every prepared food or convenience food or canned food contains salt.

> 1 lemon
> 2 cloves garlic
> 1 very small onion
> 1½ teaspoons dried basil (see p. 216)
> 1½ teaspoons dried parsley
> ¼ cup cold-pressed oil
> dash pepper
> ¼ teaspoon potassium chloride
> 1 teaspoon raw wheat germ
> ¼ teaspoon granulated kelp
> 1 teaspoon honey

Wash, peel, and pit the lemon, and liquify at high speed. Peel and halve the garlic and onion. Add to the lemon and blend at high speed until liquified. Add the rest of the ingredients and blend at low speed until smooth.
Yield: about ¾ cup.

## NUT DRESSING

Here is an unusual sweet dressing that is excellent on salads, especially fruit salads.

> ¼ cup pecans
> ¼ cup almonds
> ½ teaspoon dry mustard
> ⅛ teaspoon paprika
> ½ teaspoon sea salt
> ½ teaspoon honey
> ½ cup cold-pressed oil

Together, grind the nuts at high speed in the blender until they are a fine meal—you don't want any large pieces. Add the remaining ingredients and blend at low speed until smooth.
Yield: a little more than ½ cup.

## RUSSIANISH DRESSING

To make a real Russian Dressing you need chili peppers, and our diet, while it may encompass a little mustard, pulls up short of chilies. Otherwise, this is very like a traditional Russian Dressing.

> *1 medium tomato*
> *1/3 medium green pepper*
> *½ stalk celery*
> *1 teaspoòn dry mustard*
> *½ cup Basic Mayonnaise (see p. 86)*

Wash and quarter the tomato and liquify at high speed (you want ½ cup pulp when it's blended). Wash the pepper well, cut into 1-inch chunks, and liquify at high speed. Wash the celery and cut into 1-inch pieces, and liquify. Blend in the mustard. Pour the mixture into the Mayonnaise and stir well.
Yield: about 1½ cups.

## YOGHURT DRESSING

Yoghurt can be used as a substitute for sour cream in sour cream dressings. Blend the yoghurt as little as possible— you don't want to kill off the bacteria with the heat of the blades.

> *2 medium plum tomatoes*
> *2 tablespoons cold-pressed oil*
> *1 teaspoon granulated kelp*
> *½ teaspoon sea salt*
> *1 tablespoon vinegar*
> *1 tablespoon dried basil (see p. 216)*
> *dash or 2 pepper*
> *¾ cup fresh yoghurt*

Wash and liquify the tomatoes. Add the oil, kelp, salt, vinegar, basil, and pepper to the blender container, and blend until smooth. Add the yoghurt and blend briefly until the mixture is uniform.
Yield: almost 2 cups.

# SALADS

We're using the word "Salads" rather broadly here. Coleslaw is a Salad. Carrot Salad, of course, is a Salad. And, in the same sense, Cucumber and Zucchini Pickles are Salads. These chopped Salad dishes will usually keep well in the refrigerator, with the Slaws and Pickles improving for a few days of steeping (though they are delicious immediately).
Pickles come first simply because we are so fond of pickles. Acid foods, such as vinegar and lemon juice, are good for you. Many old recipes for regularity include them. The body's chemistry should run slightly acid, and yet the modern diet is full of base (alkaline) foods.

## CABBAGE PICKLES

This is an adaptation of a Japanese recipe, and one of our favorites. The recipe calls for letting the vinegar mixture cool for 10 minutes before pouring over the cabbage. That's because we want to pickle the cabbage, not cook it.

*2 pounds cabbage*
*4 tablespoons unhulled sesame seeds*

*1 cup vinegar*
*¼ cup honey*
*1 teaspoon sea salt*

Wash the cabbage but do not core it. Cut into wedges and then into smaller pieces. Blender chop at low speed, covered with water, 2 to 3 cups at a time. As each blenderful is chopped, pour off into a colander set in a bowl to drain, then scrape into another bowl. Reuse the water for the rest of the cabbage, then reserve for a soup or a drink. Measure the sesame seeds into a dry frying pan and toast over medium heat until they begin to jump, stirring once or twice. Mix the vinegar, honey, and salt together into a small saucepan and bring to a boil. Remove from the heat and add the seeds. Let stand for 10 minutes, then pour over the cabbage. Stir very well. Weight a dish, sit it on the cabbage, and let stand 1 to 2 hours before serving. Yield: 6 cups.

## QUICK ZUCCHINI PICKLES

This, and the following, pickle is made with pickling spices. Pickling spices are a combination of mustard seeds, dill seeds, peppercorns, red peppers, bay leaf, and other herbs. If you don't wish to use this ready-mixed stuff, make up your own with mustard seeds, dill seeds, peppercorns, and bay leaf. The problem with using peppercorns in this recipe is that they stay in the Pickle, either to be chewed or spat out. We recommend picking them out of your portion.

*2 pounds fresh zucchini*
*2 cloves garlic*
*1½ teaspoons sea salt*
*1½ teaspoons dill seed*
*1 rounded tablespoon pickling spices*
*1 cup cider vinegar*

Wash and trim the squash, and cut into 1-inch pieces. Blender chop, covered with water, at low speed, in 2 batches, with the peeled garlic. Drain well, reserving the water for another use, then scrape into a pot. Add the remaining ingredients, bring to the boil, stir, bring to the boil again, stir, and remove from the heat. Scrape the Pickles into a strainer and press with the back of a spoon to remove the excess vinegar. Spoon the Pickles into a jar, then press with the back of the spoon to express more liquid, either pouring or spooning out the liquid. These are eaten warm, but refrigerate any leftovers.

The flavored vinegar may be reused to make Quick Cucumber Pickles, or for a salad.

Yield: almost 2 cups.

## QUICK CUCUMBER PICKLES

Use Kirby cucumbers with the skins on for this recipe.

> *2 pounds cucumbers*
> *½ cup cider vinegar*
> *½ cup wine vinegar*
> *1 teaspoon sea salt*
> *1 teaspoon celery seed*
> *1 tablespoon pickling spices*

Wash and trim the cukes, cut them into 1 inch lengths, and blender chop, covered with water. Drain well and scrape into a pot. Add the remaining ingredients and bring to the boil. Remove from the heat immediately and spoon into a strainer. Press out the excess liquid and bottle the pickles, pressing again in the bottle to express even more liquid. Reserve this liquid to use again, for Pickles or salad dressing. Eat immediately or store in the refrigerator.

Yield: almost 2 cups.

## CARROT SALAD

Here's a tasty, vitamin-A filled lunch or side dish. The carrots have to be sweet, so taste them before blending.

> ½ cup walnuts
> ½ pound carrots
> ½ cup raisins
> ¼ cup Mayonnaise

Chop the walnuts coarsely in the blender at low speed, then scrape into a serving bowl. Wash and trim but do not peel, the carrots and cut into ¾-inch chunks. Put into the blender with the raisins, covered with water. Blender chop briefly, at low speed, until the carrots are coarse, then drain well in a colander or strainer set in a bowl, reserving the water for a soup or a drink. Add the carrots to the nuts. Stir in ¼ cup mayonnaise (or less, to your taste).
Yield: 2 servings.

## CHOPPED SALAD

This is a salad best served half and half with cottage cheese or yoghurt.

> ½ medium green pepper
> 1 small onion
> 2 medium Kirby cucumbers

Wash and cube the pepper. Peel and halve the onion. Wash and trim the cucumbers, and cut into 1-inch chunks. Put all into the blender and blender chop briefly at low speed, covered with water. Drain well, reserve the water for a drink. Serve the salad mixed with yoghurt or cottage cheese.
Yield: 2 servings.

## COLESLAW

How can you have a blender book without Coleslaw? It's a natural. Vary the ingredients to suit your own taste.

> 1½ pounds cabbage
> 1 carrot
> 1 green pepper
> 1 rounded tablespoon raw wheat germ
> 2 tablespoons honey
> 1 tablespoon vinegar
> 1 teaspoon celery seed
> 3-4 tablespoons Mayonnaise
> sea salt and pepper

Wash, trim and cut the cabbage into wedges, but do not core. Blender chop, covered with water, at low speed, 2 to 3 cups at a time, and drain in a colander set in a bowl. Wash and trim the carrot, and cut into 1-inch chunks, and blend with the pepper, washed and chunked. Drain the ingredients well as they are blended (save the water for soups or drinks). Add the wheat germ, honey, vinegar, and celery seed, and then add Mayonnaise and salt and pepper to taste.
This dish does not require steeping, so serve at once.
Yield: about 7 cups.

## COLESLAW II

This is a slightly sweeter Coleslaw.

> ½ medium cabbage
> 2 stalks celery
> 1 apple
> 1 teaspoon caraway seeds
> dash sea salt
> 1 tablespoon vinegar
> ¾ cup Dill-Onion Mayonnaise (see p. 89)

Wash and trim the cabbage and cut it into wedges, but do not core it. At low speed, blender chop, covered with water, in 3 batches, pouring off each batch into a colander set in a bowl to drain, reserving the water for reuse. Wash the celery (leave on the leaves) and cut into 1-inch pieces. Wash and core, but do not peel, the apple and cut it into eighths. Blender chop both in the reserved water, and drain in the same colander. Save the water for another use. Scrape the chopped ingredients into a bowl and add the caraway seeds, salt, and vinegar. Mix well. Add the Mayonnaise and mix again.
Yield: about 7 cups.

## RED CABBAGE SALAD

This is not a Slaw, except in the sense that "slaw" means salad. Red cabbage makes a pleasant change. The taste is much the same, but that purple is such a rich color that it *feels* different.

> 2 cups nutmeats
> 1 small red cabbage (about 1¼ pounds)
> ¼ cup wine vinegar
> 1 tablespoon honey
> 1 cup raisins

Blender chop the nutmeats coarse, 1 cup at a time, at low speed, and reserve in a mixing bowl. Wash and trim, but do not core, the cabbage; cut into wedges, and blender chop at low speed, covered with water, 2 or 3 cups at a time. Drain the cabbage in a colander set in a bowl, re-using the same water for each batch.
In a small saucepan simmer together for a minute the vinegar, honey, and raisins. Scrape the drained cabbage over the nutmeats. Pour the vinegar mixture over the cabbage. Mix very well and either serve immediately or store in the refrigerator.
Save the liquid for Lilac Milk, page 207.
Yield: 4 to 5 cups.

## MIXED SALAD

We like nuts in salads—or beans. Cooked soybeans would make a very pleasant variation for the nuts in this recipe. But, if you use soybeans, don't chop them.

*½ cup walnut meats*
*½ pound Kirby cucumbers*
*1 stalk celery*
*1 small green pepper*
*1 cup fresh bean sprouts*

Blender chop the walnuts at low speed, quite coarse, and reserve in a serving bowl. Blender chop together the washed and trimmed and chunked cucumber, the washed celery cut into 1-inch pieces, and the washed green pepper, chunked, covered with water. Pour off into a colander set in a bowl, reserving the blender water for soup. Scrape the vegetables out over the nuts, add the bean sprouts, and mix well.
Serve this Salad with any dressing.
Yield: more than 3 cups.

## PICKLED BEET SALAD

Beets aren't around all year, and when they are not, we miss them. This is quite a tasty way to eat them, as is the Borscht in Chapter 1. Beets have a little of most of the vitamins and minerals listed in *Composition of Foods,* USDA Handbook No. 8, but (and this is surprising for a red vegetable) no vitamin A. However, in beets there is a good deal of potassium, which is lacking in many diets (but available in many root vegetables).

*1 pound beets*
*1 teaspoon caraway seeds*
*1 cup water*
*1 cup vinegar*

*1 tablespoon honey*
*1 medium onion*

Wash, peel, and quarter the beets (cut them into smaller pieces if they are large beets). Blender chop with the caraway seeds, in the water and vinegar, then dump, water and all, into a pot. If you need a second chopping, drain the beets and seeds and reuse the same water. Add the honey to the pot, bring to the boil, and simmer for about 15 minutes—or until crisply done. Most of the liquid will have boiled off, so there's no need to drain. When the beets are cooked, chop the onion coarsely by hand and mix in (use more or less onion to taste).
Serve hot or cold as a relish or side dish.
Yield: about 3 cups.

## WALDORF SALAD

We could not find an etymology for Waldorf Salad, but it's reasonable to assume it's from the New York hotel. The dish only sounds fancy—you don't need an occasion to serve it.

*1½ cups nutmeats*
*3 medium celery stalks*
*1 large apple*
*1 small head lettuce*
*French Dressing or Mayonnaise (see p. 86–92)*

Blender chop the nutmeats, coarsely at high speed, and reserve in a serving bowl. Blender chop the celery covered with water. Drain well, and add to the nuts. (Reserve the water for a drink or soup.) Hand chop the apple, tear the lettuce apart, and add both. Mix well.
Serve well mixed with French Dressing or a Mayonnaise.
Yield: a lunch for 2.

# KETCHUPS AND SAUCE

This was a fun section to research—we still, after several months, have the last remains of Cranberry Ketchup in our refrigerator. And it's still delicious and wholesome, though it has darkened.

The Tomato Sauce is the best we ever made—so good, in fact, that we couldn't see the point of including others.

## CRANBERRY KETCHUP

Everyone who hears about this recipe seems to say, "*What ketchup?*" with an incredulous lift of the eyebrows. Well, ketchups are not all tomato. A ketchup is anything like this, chopped up, spiced up, cooked up: you could even have a plum ketchup or a grape ketchup. This really is a delightful condiment, and you will be cheating yourself of a treat if you pass it by because it sounds different.

> 1 pound cranberries
> ½ cup cider vinegar
> ½ cup water
> ¾ cup honey
> 2 tablespoons blackstrap molasses
> ½ teaspoon cinnamon
> ½ teaspoon clove
> ½ teaspoon ginger
> ½ teaspoon sea salt
> dash of pepper

Wash the cranberries well in hot water and remove any stems left on. Put into a pot with the vinegar and water, bring to a boil, and cook over medium heat for a few minutes. Allow to cool to the point where you can put your finger into the mixture, then pour into the blender,

and blend at medium speed until smooth. Add the remaining ingredients to the blender container, 1 at a time, blending at the lowest speed your machine will allow. Blend until very smooth. Pour the mixture back into the same pot and simmer gently for 5 minutes, stirring once or twice. Store in the refrigerator in glass jars.
Yield: about 1 quart.

## TOMATO-APPLE KETCHUP

This is not like commercial tomato ketchups (or catsups). Because of the blender, it is more orange than red. It's also sweeter, and less spiced. We use it on anything that's improved by Ketchup—except that we never never eat hamburgers.

> 2 tablespoons vegetable oil
> 1 pound tomatoes
> 1 medium apple
> 1 medium onion
> ½ small green pepper
> ¼ cup honey
> 1½ teaspoons sea salt
> ¼ teaspoon cinnamon
> ¼ cup vinegar

Oil a large skillet. Wash and cut the tomatoes into chunks; wash and core, but do not peel, the apple and cut it into chunks; peel and hand chop the onion. Put these ingredients into the skillet and cook over a medium-high flame until the onions are transparent. Remove from the heat and allow to cool for a few minutes, then pour into the blender. Process at low speed until smooth. Wash and chunk the green pepper and add to the blender container. Then add the honey, salt, cinnamon, and vinegar. Process until very smooth.
Store in the refrigerator in glass or plastic jars.
Yield: a bit less than 1 quart.

## TOMATO KETCHUP

2 tablespoons vegetable oil
2 pounds tomatoes
1 medium onion
1 small green pepper
2 teaspoons sea salt
½ teaspoon ground cloves
1/16 teaspoon pepper
1 tablespoon honey
¼ cup vinegar

Oil a large skillet. Wash and chunk the tomatoes. Peel and chop the onion by hand. Cook both in the skillet over medium-high heat, covered, until the onion is transparent. Remove from the heat and allow to cool. Blend at low speed until smooth. Wash and chunk the green pepper, and blend in. Blend in the remaining ingredients until quite smooth.
Store in glass or plastic in the refrigerator.
Yield: less than 1 quart.

## TOMATO SAUCE

Here's a dish that speaks for itself.

2 tablespoons vegetable oil
2 large cloves garlic
½ pound onions
2 pounds tomatoes
1 teaspoon fennel seed
2 teaspoons dried basil (see p. 216)
2 teaspoons oregano
1 teaspoon sea salt

Oil a large skillet. Peel, chunk, and blender chop the garlic and onions into coarse bits, covered with water. Drain well.

(Squeeze the water out with the bottom of a bowl pressed into the colander, and reserve for another use.) Cook, covered, in the skillet over a medium flame until the onion begins to brown. Wash and cut the tomatoes into sixteenths, and add to the skillet with the rest of the ingredients. Increase heat to high, and cook for 7 minutes, stirring once or twice. Remove from the heat and allow to cool. Blend at medium speed until smooth, then reheat carefully in the same skillet.

Yield: enough sauce for ½ pound of pasta (3½ cups).

# DIPS AND SPREADS

Spreads are thicker and dips are thinner—and that's the difference. They are both well-suited to the blender.

Dips can often be blended without any help from your spatula, the liquid in the recipe being enough to keep everything moving. Spreads always need help from your spatula; you'll blend briefly, then shut off the machine and push the ingredients back down onto the blades. This means that spreads are a bit more work, but they are well worth it.

Don't think that Dips and Spreads are just party-time things. With your blender they can brighten almost any meal.

Dips and Spreads should be stored in the refrigerator, in small glass or plastic jars.

# YOGHURT DIPS

The beneficial bacteria in yoghurt (and that's mostly what we eat it for) live and die on a rising and falling curve. The first day or so the curve of the amount of beneficial bacteria rises, reaching a peak and staying there on the fourth to sixth days. After the sixth day the benefit we derive from the yoghurt falls sharply. So, yoghurt should be eaten fresh, preferably within a week of starting it. But with commercial yoghurt you can never be certain of its age. The only way to have surely fresh yoghurt is to make it yourself. It is a very simple process requiring a warm spot, some commercial yoghurt or yoghurt starter, water, and powdered milk (or any form of milk, including soy milk or Cashew Milk). See page 215 for the complete recipe.

There are other benefits to eating yoghurt, besides the bacteria. Yoghurt is a good source of protein—in *pre-digested* form. For so many people uncultured milk is difficult to digest, while yoghurt (and cheese) is easily assimilated. Also, because it is acid, the calcium it contains is readily absorbed—much more readily than the calcium in uncultured milk.

Blend the yoghurt, which usually goes in last, as little as possible. The blending process loosens the yoghurt, making it thinner; but more important, the heat of the blender blades can kill off the beneficial bacteria—half defeating our purpose in eating yoghurt.

## TOMATO YOGHURT DIP

Here's a tasy start with yoghurt dips.
To drain the liquified tomato, pour it into a strainer set
over a bowl. The pulp is still too large to go through the
strainer holes and a liquid will drip out. Drink the tomato
juice or save it for a soup.

> ¼ pound tomatoes
> 1 teaspoon granulated kelp
> 1 teaspoon dried basil (see p. 216)
> 1 small clove garlic
> ½ cup yoghurt (see p. 215)

Wash and trim the tomato, cut into quarters, and liquify
at high speed in the blender. Strain, as described above,
then return the pulp to the blender. Add the kelp, basil,
and garlic and blend until the garlic is chopped. Stir in the
yoghurt with your spatula, then blend briefly to make
smooth.
Yield: ¾ cup.
To make TOMATO COTTAGE CHEESE DIP, add 1 teaspoon
oregano with the basil, and substitute cottage cheese for
the yoghurt.

## DILL DIP

Fresh dill is readily available at both large supermarkets
in our neighborhood. Dill is difficult to grow in an apartment because it grows rather tall for an herb.

> ½ cup yoghurt (see p. 215)
> ½ cup cottage cheese
> handful fresh dill (1/3-½ ounce)

Measure the yoghurt and cottage cheese into the blender.
Wash the dill well, towel it dry, and cut it into 1-inch
pieces. Blend until all the dill is chopped.
Yield: 1 cup.

## VEGETABLE YOGHURT DIP

Here's a dip that's as nutritious as a vegetable dinner. There's a little vitamin A in the scallion, a little vitamin C in the pepper, iodine and calcium in the kelp, and calcium and B vitamins in the yoghurt, as well as many other minerals and traces of vitamins—if all the ingredients are fresh.

> 1 small Kirby cucumber
> ½ small green pepper
> 1 scallion
> 1 teaspoon kelp
> 1 small clove garlic
> ½ teaspoon fennel seeds
> pinch thyme
> ½ cup yoghurt (see p. 215)

Wash and trim the Kirby cucumber but do not peel it. Cut into ½-inch pieces and grind by dropping through the opening in your blender cover, with the motor going at medium speed. Scrub and pit the pepper, cut it up, and blend the same way. Wash and cut the scallion into 1-inch pieces and blend in. Add the kelp, garlic, fennel seed, and thyme and blend. Stir in the yoghurt, and blend briefly. Yield: more than 1 cup.

## RAISIN DIP

Raisins, being dried fruit, will absorb liquid from the yoghurt and make this more solid than most yoghurt dips. It is a sweet dip, and reminiscent of filling for cannoli, especially in the cottage cheese variation, given below.

> ½ cup raisins
> ½ cup yoghurt (see p. 215)

Blend the raisins at medium speed until most are chopped. Add the yoghurt and blend briefly to mix thoroughly. Set aside for an hour or so to set. Yield: about ¾ cup.

## COTTAGE CHEESE RAISIN DIP

> ½ cup raisins
> ½ cup cottage cheese
> 1 teaspoon vanilla (see p. 215)

Blend the raisins until mostly chopped, then add the cottage cheese and vanilla and blend until the curds are reduced in size. Help the cottage cheese onto the blades with your spatula. May be served immediately.
Yield: almost a cup.

## YOGHURT-PINEAPPLE DIP

Pineapple will act like apple if given the chance: that is, it will liquify when you have enough in the blender. The amount of pineapple called for is about half a large pineapple, trimmed.

> 1 pound pineapple meat
> 2 teaspoons dried mint leaves (see p. 216)
> ½ cup yoghurt (see p. 215)

Wash and peel the pineapple well. Cut it into chunks and drop 1 at a time through the opening in your blender top at high speed. When liquified, add the mint leaves and blend for another few seconds. Add the yoghurt, stir in with your spatula, and blend briefly at low speed.
Yield: 2¼ cups.

# VEGETARIAN DIPS

Vegetarian dishes are their own justification; and vegetable dips have their full nutritional value in a very attractive form.

## BABA GHANNOUJ

This Lebanese eggplant dip (pronounced bah-bah-guh-noosh rapidly, as if it were one word) is a real treat and a surprise for those who expect any eggplant dish to be bitter.

> 2 eggplants
> 2 lemons
> ½ cup vegetable oil
> 1 rounded teaspoon sea salt
> 2 large cloves garlic

Wash, trim, and split the eggplants in half, lengthwise. Lay the halves face down on an ungreased baking sheet and, starting in a cold oven, bake at 400° to 450° for about 45 minutes, or until the skin is crisp.

Wash and pit the lemons and blend at high speed until in tiny bits. When the eggplants are done (the flesh should be very soft), remove from the oven and cool until you can handle them. With a spoon, scrape the flesh out of the eggplant skins and into the blender with the lemon. Blend at high speed until liquified. Add the oil and salt. Peel and add the garlic cloves; blend until creamy.

Serve with *crudités* of raw cauliflower, cucumber, and the like.

Yield: almost 2 cups.

## GUACAMOLE

Here is a gem of a dish, smooth, creamy, and delicious. In buying avocado for Guacamole, buy one that has gone soft, but is not all brown. The hard green ones are attractive, but not sweet because they are unripe. Don't be frightened off by the "health food" ingredients in the Dip; you won't be able to distinguish them in the delicious taste of the whole.

> 1 large lemon
> 1 large ripe avocado

>*4 tablespoons cold-pressed oil*
>*2 cloves garlic*
>*1 small onion*
>*dash or 2 pepper*
>*¼ teaspoon sea salt*
>*¼ teaspoon granulated kelp*
>*2 teaspoons raw wheat germ*
>*1 teaspoon eating yeast*

Wash, peel, and pit the lemon, and blend at high speed until liquified. Wash the avocado, split it, and spoon out the flesh into the blender (save the pit for growing). Measure in the oil and blend until smooth. Peel the garlic cloves and onion, cut in half, and blend until smooth. Add the pepper, salt, kelp, wheat germ, and eating yeast, and blend again, until smooth.

For a spicier Dip, add a dash or 2 of red pepper flakes.

Yield: about 1¼ cups. Serve with cucumber or celery spears.

## PEPPER DIP

Ripe green peppers (which are red and sweet) have the highest vitamin C content of any fresh vegetable—higher than any citrus fruit, too. Even green they have more vitamin C than citrus. If you can get them, use *all* sweet red peppers.

>*1 pound mixed green and red sweet peppers*
>*1 teaspoon granulated kelp*
>*½ teaspoon Dill Salt (see p. 135)*

Scrub the peppers well and core and trim them. Cut into eighths and liquify (without water) in the blender at highest speed. Pour the liquid peppers into a strainer set in a bowl, and allow to drain (the water is extremely rich in vitamins, so don't throw it away). Scrape the peppers back into the blender and add the kelp and Dill Salt. Blend until well mixed.

Yield: 1 cup.

## MUSHROOM DIP

Mushrooms, it seems, are always expensive nowadays, but here is one delicious Dip that is worth the money. *Don't overcook the mushrooms*—they are at their tastiest when they just change color.

> 2 tablespoons vegetable oil
> 1 medium onion
> 1 pound mushrooms
> 1 teaspoon sea salt
> ⅛ teaspoon pepper
> 1 10 minute egg

Oil a large skillet. Peel the onion, and coarsely hand chop. Sauté over high heat until transparent. Brush off the mushrooms with a towel to clean them, then cut off the hard ends. If the mushrooms are small, do not slice. If medium-sized, cut in half lengthwise. If they are large, slice lengthwise into 4 or more slices. Dump the entire pound into the skillet with the onions, lower the flame to medium, and cook, covered, for a few minutes, until the mushrooms begin to change their color to a deeper brown. When cooked, remove from the heat and allow to cool for a few minutes. Spoon the mushrooms and onion into the blender with a slotted spoon (you don't want the dip too wet). Add the salt, pepper, and the hard-boiled egg, quartered. Blend as little as you can and still have everything well mixed. Yield: about 1½ cups.
For VEGETARIAN CHOPPED LIVER, add 2 rounded tablespoons eating yeast to the recipe.

## LOW-CAL ZUCCHINI DIP

Any dip that contains no oil or sweetener has to be low calorie. There are no more than 40 calories in this dish, which is probably fewer calories than you burn in making and eating it.

*½ pound zucchini*
*½ teaspoon Dill Salt (see p. 135)*

Wash and trim the squash, cutting away the hard ends only. Cut into ½-inch slices and drop 1 at a time through the hole in the blender top, with the motor going at high speed, until almost liquified. Help with your spatula when necessary. Add the salt and blend in.
Just before serving, scrape into a strainer and allow the liquid expressed by the squash to drain out.
Yield: 1 cup.

# MEAT SPREADS

Animal protein contains essential amino acids. These amino acids are the building blocks of the body. For a long time there has been a running battle between the traditional and the "health food" nutritionists about the necessity for animal protein (which is, by the way, available in eggs and milk products too). Amino acids are also available in legumes, especially in soybeans. So, a strict vegetarian can have a balanced diet, with care.
We are not complete vegetarians, but the number of meat recipes in this book reflects the amount of meat we eat in our lives. We are, I suppose, (and certainly in comparison with the "average" American) partial vegetarians, in that the vast bulk of our diet is made up of vegetables, fruits, nuts, and seeds. We take some animal protein most days (unless we are eating soybeans), but usually as eggs and milk products.
We did not come to this diet suddenly, with all we now know about our own nutritional needs full-blown. We arrived at this predominately vegetarian diet a little at a time—and we feel that is the best route. A sudden detour to an all vegetable diet will get the backs of any family up—especially if they have been used to lots of meat in their diet. Moderation is the key.

Now, all of this may sound as if we are putting down the recipes that follow—not at all. We do eat some meat, fish, and poultry, and that is reflected here. An occasional meat dish is good for variety.

## CHICKEN PÂTÉ

If you don't want to bother making the Pâté (it is a very good filling for Wheat Germ Crepes: see page 78), the cooked chicken and sauce make an excellent main dish over brown rice or Noodles (see pages 47 and 48). Whenever you cook chicken, throw away the skin and trim off the fat. The skin is a good deal fat, and pesticide residues tend to concentrate in fat. In addition, animal fats tend to be rather highly saturated.

> ¼ cup almond nutmeats
> 2 tablespoons vegetable oil
> 3-pound chicken
> ¼ cup tamari soy sauce
> 2 tablespoons wine
> ½ teaspoon garlic powder, or more, to taste

Grind the nutmeats coarsely in the blender at high speed and reserve them. Oil a large skillet. Trim the skinned meat from the breast, legs, and thighs of the chicken (save the bones and wings for soup). Cut into 1 inch pieces and put in the skillet. Add the tamari, wine (we use dry vermouth; it is cheap and leaves a nice flavor because of its herbs), and sprinkle the garlic powder over all. Turn the heat on high and sauté for a *few minutes,* uncovered, stirring and turning where needed, until the chicken is just done. Taste to make sure it is done, but don't overcook or it will get dry. Remove from the heat and allow to cool for a few minutes. With a fork, pick out pieces of chicken and drop through the hole in the blender top, with the machine going at highest speed, until all ground. Add 3 tablespoons of the cooking sauce, tasting the mixture after each tablespoonful. Add the nuts and blend until well distributed. Yield: about 1 cup.

## CHICKEN HEART PÂTÉ

We like chicken hearts. You might, too, if you gave them a chance. Most nutritionists consider organ meats superior to muscle meat.

>*½ pound chicken hearts*
>*1 small onion*
>*¼ teaspoon Sage Salt (see p. 136)*
>*pinch ground leaf sage (see p. 216)*
>*⅛ teaspoon ground bay leaf (see p. 216)*
>*1 tablespoon wine*

Trim the fat from the chicken hearts (like inactive people, chickens who just sit in a chicken house get fat around their hearts), and dump into an ungreased skillet. Peel and dice the onion and put in the skillet. Sauté over medium heat, stirring occasionally for about 5 minutes. Remove from the heat and allow to cool for 5 minutes.
Spoon through your blender top (with the motor at low speed) 2 tablespoons at a time. When all chopped coarsely, add the salt, sage, bay, and wine, and stir with your spatula. At low speed, alternately process and stir with the spatula until a thick and smooth consistency.
Yield: 1 cup.

## FISH SPREAD

This recipe also makes a good Crepes filling. The fish we use most often is turbot. We find it in all our local supermarkets, frozen, filleted, and ready to use. It is a very white, sweet fish, with a delicate flavor excellent for just broiling.

>*2 tablespoons vegetable oil*
>*1 large onion*
>*1 pound filleted fish*
>*1 teaspoon dill seed*
>*dash sea salt*
>*2 small scallions*

Oil a large skillet. Peel and coarsely hand chop the onion, and put it into the skillet. Cut the fish into 1-inch cubes, dump in the skillet, and add the dill seed and salt. Sauté, uncovered, stirring occasionally, until the fish is *barely done*, only a few minutes. Remove from the heat and allow to cool for a few minutes. Spoon everything into the blender, and blend at the lowest possible speed, shutting off the motor and helping the mixture with your spatula as needed. When smooth, trim the scallions, cut into 1-inch pieces, and blend in.
Yield: more than a cup of Spread.

## LIVER SPREAD

Chopped liver is supposed to be a little coarser than this, so call it a spread—but the ingredients are, with some adaptation, traditional for chopped liver.

> *1 tablespoon vegetable oil*
> *1 medium-small onion*
> *½ pound chicken livers*
> *½ teaspoon sea salt*
> *2 dashes pepper*
> *1 10-minute egg*

Oil a small skillet. Peel and hand chop the onion coarsely, and sauté until transparent. Add the livers and cook *briefly* over medium heat until just done. Liver is most unpalatable when it is overcooked. Remove the livers from the heat when done and allow to cool for a few minutes. Drop into the blender 1 at a time, with the motor going at high speed. Shut it off. Scrape in the onions and add the salt, pepper, and the hard-boiled egg, cut in quarters. Blend until smooth.
Yield: 1½ cups.

## HERBED LIVER SPREAD

Liver is an excellent food, there is no better source of
B vitamins (not even eating yeast). But many people find
it unpalatable. Here's a recipe for people who hate liver.
We tried it out on the fiercest liver hater we know, and
his eyes lifted and he gobbled.

>    *1 tablespoon vegetable oil*
>    *1 small onion*
>    *1 clove garlic*
>    *¼ teaspoon savory*
>    *¼ teaspoon thyme*
>    *½ pound chicken livers*
>    *dashes sea salt and pepper*

Oil a small skillet. Peel and coarsely hand chop the onion
and garlic. Sauté with the savory and thyme until the onion
is transparent. Add the livers and cook over medium heat
until just done. Remove the skillet from the heat and allow
the livers to cool for a few minutes. Blend by dropping in
1 at a time, with the motor going at high speed. Blend in
salt and pepper to taste.
Yield: 1 cup.

## TONGUE SPREAD

Organ meats tend to have less protein but more vitamins
and minerals than the more ordinary cuts of meat.

>    *1 cup cooked lean tongue (2 slices ½ by 4 inches)*
>    *2 tablespoons Quick Cucumber Pickles (see p. 98)*
>                   *or*
>    *½ medium sour pickle*

(If you use the sour pickle instead of the already chopped
Quick Cucumber Pickles, cut the sour pickle into ½-inch
slices and chop in blender. If you use 2 tablespoons Quick
Cucumber Pickles, process the tongue first.) Trim and cube
the tongue, then drop 1 or 2 cubes at a time through the

opening in the blender cap. When coarsely chopped, add
the Quick Cucumber Pickles and blend in.
Refrigerate and serve cold.
Yield: ½ to ¾ cup.

# CHEESE SPREADS

Cheese Spreads always have to be helped through the
blender with your spatula—they are too thick to process
on their own.
We like to use sharp cheeses for spreads—preferably sharp,
uncolored cheddar. Mild cheeses seem to wind up with
almost no flavor at all in a spread.
Cheese is a very good food, except for the butterfat content. Its protein is more readily digested than plain milk
protein.
Except for those cheeses specifically marked salt free, all
cheeses are made with salt and a solidifying agent. So, if
you are on a salt-free diet, be warned. Also, no cheese is
naturally that yellow-orange color of American cheese.
That color is achieved by adding dye, as is the reddish rind
of Muenster cheese. But we can't tell you just what dye, or
what other chemicals are in your American cheese or
processed cheese. Cheese is another Standard of Identity
food, which means that the federal government protects
the manufacturer from your knowing the precise additives
he uses. Also, when processed cheeses and cheese spreads
are made commercially, the maker adds water, chemicals,
and fillers. So, for your pocketbook *and* your health, start
with natural cheeses and make your own spreads.

## PLAIN CHEESE SPREAD

Don't try this recipe, or any of these Cheese Spreads, if
you can't remove the base of your blender. Cheese Spreads
are thick, and difficult to scrape out with the base on.

*¼ pound uncolored cheddar cheese*
*2 tablespoons milk*

Cut the cheese into ½-inch chunks and feed through the opening in the blender top one at a time, with the motor at medium speed, until ground. Add the milk and, using a rubber spatula, push the mixture onto the blender blades repeatedly until smooth and creamy. Remember don't put your spatula into the container with the motor on.
Yield: ½ cup.

To make a WINE SPREAD, substitute cream sherry for the milk—or any wine you like. It will be much better than commercial wine spreads, which are invariably made with too much salt.

## ONION-CHEESE SPREAD

If you'd like to, substitute 2 tablespoons of onion flakes or dried onion for the fresh onion. If you do, increase the beer by ½ tablespoon, and let the dip sit around for a couple of hours to soak up the liquid. Using fresh onion is simpler.

*1 tablespoon beer*
*1 small raw onion*
*¼ pound uncolored cheddar cheese*

Measure the beer into the blender. Peel the onion and quarter it. Turn the machine on to medium speed and drop the quarters, 1 at a time, through the opening in the blender top. Cut the cheese into ¾-inch chunks, and blend them similarly. Help the cheese onto the blades with your spatula.
Don't double this recipe—cheese is difficult stuff to blend.
Yield: about ½ cup.

## CARAWAY-CHEESE SPREAD

Ever wonder how they manufacture caraway cheese? Very much the way you will make it here. Cheese (often Meunster) is watered into a kind of paste, the seeds are added, and it is reset. Except that when the commercial makers go through this process, they usually add chemicals to make the cheese creamier. We like caraway cheese very much, and we never have to buy it with chemicals.

> *3 tablespoons beer*
> *2 teaspoons caraway seeds*
> *¼ pound uncolored cheddar cheese*

Measure the beer and seeds into the blender. Chunk the cheese into ¾-inch pieces and feed, 1 at a time, with the motor at medium speed, through the opening in your blender top, until all are ground. Help the cheese onto the blender blades with your spatula. if necessary.
Allow to stand a while before serving to let the caraway seeds soften.
Yield: about ½ cup.

## GARLIC SPREAD

Garlic Spread can be made with either fresh or powdered garlic. The fresh garlic has the advantage of containing garlic oil, and garlic oil is supposed to be helpful in keeping away colds (as well as vampires). However, a spread made with fresh garlic is not at its best until the next day, while a spread made with powdered garlic is ready to eat immediately.

> *¼ pound sharp uncolored cheddar cheese*
> *1 medium clove garlic*
> *or*
> *½ teaspoon powdered garlic*
> *2½ tablespoons milk*

Cut the cheese into ½-inch chunks and drop through the opening in your blender cap 1 at a time, with the motor at medium speed, until all are ground. Peel, quarter, and add the fresh garlic (or measure in the powdered) add the milk, and help with the spatula until all is ground well. Turn the motor off whenever you poke the spatula in.
Yield: ½ cup.

## CHEDDAR-PICKLE SPREAD

This recipe calls for a sour pickle because our Quick Cucumber and Quick Zucchini Pickles are not sour enough. Buy only fresh pickles, the kind that are kept in the refrigerator case of your supermarket, and read the ingredients on the label: some fresh pickles contain undesirable chemicals.

> ¼ pound uncolored cheddar cheese
> 1 medium-small sour pickle

Cut the cheese and the pickle into ¾-inch chunks, put into the blender, and blend at high speed. Shut the motor off and push the mixture onto the blades with your spatula. Turn the blender on, and repeat until the pickle is well distributed—but not ground fine.
Yield: a bit more than ½ cup.

## SWISS-PARMESAN SPREAD

Parmesan has a very strong taste; we balance that with the milder Swiss. Even so, this is a spread that the kids will find too sharp. Do you wonder why we use beer as a liquid in some of our spreads? It has some flavor of its own. However, any liquid would do, so long as it didn't conflict with the cheeses—even the juice that is sometimes left when we liquify vegetables for dips.

*⅛ pound domestic Swiss cheese*
*¼ cup beer*
*⅛ pound grated Parmesan cheese*

Cut the Swiss into ½-inch chunks and grind by dropping, 1 at a time, through the opening of your blender top with the motor at high speed. Add the beer and the Parmesan, and blend well, helping the cheese onto the blades with a spatula when needed.
Yield: about ½ cup.

## CHEESE YOGHURT SPREAD

Even the small amount of yoghurt in this recipe helps us to absorb the calcium in the cheese. And both yoghurt and cheese are sources of readily available protein. This spread comes out a little thinner than the preceding recipes.

*¼ pound uncolored cheddar cheese*
*2 heaping tablespoons fresh yoghurt (see p. 215)*
*1 heaping tablespoon raw wheat germ*

Cut the cheddar into ¾-inch chunks and grind in the blender by dropping the cubes in 1 at a time, with the motor going at medium speed. Spoon in the remaining ingredients and blend as briefly as you can and still get it smooth.
Yield: a little more than ½ cup.

# SESAME SPREADS

Sesame seeds are quite popular in the Middle East, and quite popular among nutrition-minded Westerners, too. Most seeds are rich in vitamins and minerals, but sesame seeds are especially rich (they even have B vitamins), and by weight contain 8 to 10 times the calcium of whole milk. All of this makes sesame seeds an excellent food. These seeds do not grind very easily in the blender; it is often necessary to stop the machine and use the spatula to help them onto the blender blades. And, to be truthful, we have never been able, in the blender, to get as much oil out of the seeds as we would like for sesame butter or plain tahini.

Of course, we use only sesame seeds with the hulls on. They are not quite as sweet as the hulled seeds, but *the hulls guarantee freshness.*

There is also available a decorticated sesame seed, but don't use it. This is equivalent to degerminating cornmeal —the vitamin E is largely in the cortex (the germ). When decorticated, there is little or no vitamin E left.

## LEMON TAHINI

This popular Middle-Eastern spread can be eaten by itself, or on a whole grain cracker, or on a spinach or lettuce leaf. Plain water is called for in this recipe, but feel free to substitute fresh vegetable cooking water—so long as it isn't salty—or blender water.

> 1 cup sesame seeds
> ¼ cup water
> 2 large cloves garlic
> 1 lemon
> 1 teaspoon sea salt
> few drops vinegar
> 2 tablespoons cold-pressed oil

Measure the seeds into your blender container and grind at low speed until the motor labors, then increase the speed until the seeds are finely ground. Add the water, peel and quarter the garlic, peel and seed the lemon, and add to the blender. Grind all at high speed until the garlic disappears. Add the salt, vinegar, and oil, and blend at medium speed until smooth.

Yield: more than a cup.

## TAHINI-ONION SPREAD

A commercial variety of this spread is available in New York. It is more pungent because it is made with *miso,* a fermented barley and soy sauce condiment. Tamari, which is an aged soy sauce, does the trick for us.

> *¾ cup sesame seeds*
> *2 teaspoons cold-pressed oil*
> *1 small onion*
> *1 teaspoon tamari*

Grind the seeds in the blender, starting at lowest speed and increasing speed as the motor labors. When ground finely, add the oil, and blend in. Peel and quarter the onion, and blend in until in small pieces, not tiny bits. Blend the tamari in briefly.
Yield: about 1 cup.

## SESAME PICKLE SPREAD

> *¾ cup sesame seeds*
> *4 tablespoons Quick Cucumber Pickles*
> *or*
> *1 medium sour pickle*

Blend the sesame seeds as on page 127 until ground quite small. Add the Pickles (or cut the sour pickle into quarters and add) and blend in until uniform. The bits of pickle should not disappear.
Yield: ½ cup.

## SESAME GARLIC SPREAD

This recipe has a unique flavor that children will probably dislike. Keep it for the adults. The wine can be any type, sweet or dry—though we find the dry more appropriate.

1 cup sesame seeds
2 tablespoons wine
2 cloves garlic
1 teaspoon Tamari

Blend the sesame seeds as on page 127 until ground well. Add the wine, and blend in. Peel and halve the garlic and add with the tamari. Blend until the garlic is well distributed. Allow to sit overnight out of the refrigerator before serving.
Yield: about ¾ cup.

# SWEET SPREADS

Not all Dips and Spreads are for appetizers—some are for desserts or candy. Here are a few that you'll want to try for children and adults both.

## PLAIN WHIPPED HONEY

Whipped honey is quite expensive in supermarkets, and none of it is "organic" honey. (Organic honey has not been heated past about 140° to get it out of the comb, and it is from flowers and bees that haven't been sprayed.) So, here's a way to turn your own organic honey into a great spread for any one of the Griddle Cakes in Chapter 2.

1 cup honey

Drip the honey into the blender with the motor going at low speed. As the honey thickens and more is dripped in, you'll want to shift to higher speeds. Stop blending when the machine sounds like it's going to throw a fit. Refrigerate to make even thicker (though honey never needs refrigeration to keep).

## APRICOT WHIPPED HONEY

This is our favorite. We make it with unsulfured apricots that have been sun dried. They look terribly dark and dry but they taste grand and have all their vitamins intact. That marvelous color on the fruit in candy shops is the result of bleaching.

> *2 ounces dried apricots*
> *1 cup honey*

Wash the apricots in hot water and soak for about 5 minutes. Reserving the liquid to drink, grind the apricots until fine by dropping 1 at a time through the blender top with the motor going at medium speed. Add the honey, dripping it in, starting at low speed and working up as your blender labors, until the honey is quite thick. This delicious spread will thicken as the apricots soak up liquid from the honey.
Yield: a bit more than 1 cup.

## RAW PEANUT BUTTER

Not only is this Peanut Butter raw, but it also has nothing in it but peanuts. Those who like raw (unroasted) peanuts are going to love it. A more traditional kind of Peanut Butter follows on the next page.

> *1 cup raw peanuts*

Measure the peanuts, papers and all, into the blender; start blending at low speed and increase speed when the motor labors. You'll have to turn the motor off from time to time to scrape the bottom of the mixture up with your spatula. Continue to grind until the natural oil of the peanuts is expressed.
Scrape into a plastic box and press down to fill the corners. Refrigerate what you don't use immediately. Nuts in the shell, seeds in the hull, grains in the bran, all keep almost

indefinitely; but once the coverings are removed and the foods are ground, they must be refrigerated.
Yield: about ¾ cup.

To make a MOLASSES RAW BUTTER, add 2 teaspoons of blackstrap molasses late in the blending. This will help hold it together as well as sweetening.

For CAROB DIPPED PEANUT SQUARES: mix together 4 tablespoons carob flour and 2½ tablespoons water, either by hand or in the blender, cut the Raw Peanut Butter into cubes, and dip into the carob. Set on wax paper to dry overnight.

## PEANUT BUTTER

This is a good, traditional-tasting Peanut Butter, but it won't be as sweet as the supermarket kind: supermarket peanut butters are usually made with sugar. You may add 1 teaspoon of honey if you want to come closer to commercial sweetness.
Supermarket peanut butter is hydrogenated; that is, the fat molecules are saturated with hydrogen, which means that they cannot be used by your body to make chains of essential fatty acids. Food processors hydrogenate the peanut butter so that it may be stored without refrigeration. Yours must be refrigerated.
For making Butter from roasted peanuts, buy peanuts still in the shell—they keep best that way. Do not use canned salted nuts—salted nuts are often slightly (or more than slightly) rancid, and the rancidity is hidden by the salt. Buy peanuts in the shell and shell them as you need them.

> 1 cup roasted peanuts
> 1 tablespoon vegetable oil
> dash sea salt

Shell enough nuts to make 1 cup nutmeats, but keep the papers on. Grind the nuts (they're really not nuts but legumes) as in the recipe for Raw Peanut Butter. When ground, add the oil and salt and blend until smooth.
Yield: about ¾ cup.

# SALTS

Americans eat too much salt, and it's bad for us. Too much salt affects the water balance of the cells, and can kick off some inner-ear problems—which again is a question of liquid balance.

Every person with a circulation or heart problem is put on a salt-free diet. Why should we wait for these sicknesses to reduce the salt in our diet?

This is not to say that all Americans use their saltshakers too freely—though many do. Rather, the American way of eating, with processed and prepared foods, with frank-furters and potato chips, with soup mixes and cake mixes—all of which are loaded with added salt—leads to an un-aware ingestion of very large amounts of salt. There is salt in virtually every canned food, even sweet foods. There is salt in every cake mix, every candy, every processed meat —the list could cover the page. And how do you calculate the amount of salt (sodium chloride or other sodium com-pounds) you get from these foods? The fact of the matter is that you can use absolutely not one grain of salt from your saltshaker, and still be hypertensive from too much salt in your diet—if you eat large amounts of processed foods.

So, what's to do? Well, one of the purposes of this book, in case you hadn't noticed, is to provide alternatives for many of these processed foods—such as mayonnaises, ketchups, ice cream, instant soups, vegetable juices, and so on. Not that we don't use some salt in our recipes, too, we do—but always in *much* smaller amounts than will be found in the commercial counterparts, many of which are Standard of Identity foods and so don't even have to list their ingredients on their labels.

The recipes in this chapter are for herb salts, combinations of herbs and coarse salt, designed to bring out more flavor with less salt.

Coarse unrefined salt is a pure sodium chloride, without any of the several chemicals that supermarket salt makers add to *their* product to keep it white, iodized, noncaking, and free flowing. Iodine is necessary to health; the other ingredients are necessary to marketing—or so the manufacturers think. Coarse unrefined mined salt is also free of the magnesium carbonate with which sea salt is marketed to keep *it* free-flowing (though, actually, the magnesium carbonate makes magnesium available to the body—and the body needs magnesium). The coarse salt dug up from the salt mines is grayish in color and comes in large rough crystals.

Don't expect these herb salts to taste like their commercial counterparts (when they have commercial counterparts)—ours have a much higher proportion of herb, and, since you make up only a little at a time, have fresher flavor.

Let the recipes in this section suggest other herbs to you: the chives or rosemary from your windowsill pot, for example.

Using these herb salts can help you reduce the amount of salt you take in, which will, in turn, accustom you to less salt, which will help to rehabilitate some of your taste sensitivity lost from the use of too much salt.

## CELERY SALT

Perhaps, when you were a child, your father used celery salt to reactivate the bubbles in his beer. Today, beers have better heads so the celery salt can come back to the kitchen.
The last brand of celery salt we looked at had calcium stearate as a third ingredient. How about yours?
Don't grind more of any seed than you'll use in a couple of months; the seeds won't spoil, but their flavor will deteriorate if stored for a long time.

> 1 heaping tablespoon celery seed
> 2 heaping tablespoons unrefined coarse salt

Spoon the seeds into the blender and process at highest speed until ground quite fine—probably about 30 seconds When fine, add the salt and process at high speed until the salt is as fine as you want it.
Store in a small jar with a tight lid.
Yield: 1 shakerful.

## DILL SALT

We've been doing some label reading (and we hope that you do, too—and not just for herb salts): one well-known dill salt contains MSG and dextrose; another sugar and MSG (much the same thing); yet another, sugar, MSG, and cornstarch.

> 1 rounded tablespoon dill seed
> 2 rounded tablespoons unrefined coarse salt

Grind the dill seed fine at highest speed; add the salt and repeat.
Store in a small jar with a tight lid. This salt is especially great over cucumber spears.
Yield: one shakerful.

## HIGH IODINE SALT

Sea salt has no iodine left to speak of after it is refined out of sea water (though some experts think it does), and coarse-mined salt has no iodine ever. Dulse and all sea-weeds are good sources of iodine, which gets harder and harder to have in our diet as large sea fish are removed from the market as unsafe. If the amount of seaweed seems a lot for a little salt, it is—but then, us hypothyroid types need a lot of iodine and little salt, because we already tend to be water retentive.
If you wish to iodize any of the other recipes in this chapter, just add a teaspoon of ground dulse or granulated kelp.

>   *½ ounce dulse*
>   *1 tablespoon unrefined coarse salt*

Briefly grind the dulse at high speed until fine. Add the salt and grind again at high speed until fine.
Store in a small jar with a tight lid.
Yield: a half shakerful.

## SAGE SALT

This is truly unusual, because sage, aside from having such a distinctive flavor, has just a little bite, so that it seems peppery—without actually being a spice. Preferably, use leaf sage, rather than rubbed or ground sage. Even if you don't grow your own sage (and it's very easy), the leaf is much cheaper than the ground or rubbed, and a few seconds in the blender gives it a perfect texture.

>   *1 heaping tablespoon leaf sage (see p. 216)*
>   *1 heaping tablespoon unrefined salt*

Process the sage briefly at high speed, until ground, then add the salt and grind to the desired texture.
Store in a small jar with a tight lid.
Yield: half a shakerful.

## MUSHROOM SALT

This Salt has no commercial counterpart, and we can't imagine why, except for the expense of dried mushrooms. The flavor is so unusual that you often need no sauce or ketchup or other dressing for a food, just a sprinkling of Mushroom Salt. As for the dill, we get it from our neighborhood supermarket and dry it ourselves.

> 2 tablespoons dried dill weed (see p. 216)
> 1 tablespoon dried mushrooms
> 1 tablespoon unrefined coarse salt

Grind the dill weed and mushrooms together at high speed until the mushrooms are fine. Add the salt and grind, still at high speed, until the desired texture.
Store in a small jar with a tight lid.
Yield: a shakerful.

## VEGETABLE SALT

Here's a Salt with more ingredients and a different flavor. If you find some of the ingredients hard to come by, improvise.
Folks on salt-free diets can substitute 2 teaspoons of potassium chloride for the tablespoon of coarse salt (making this "salt" entirely from potassium chloride). Salt-freers are allowed potassium chloride because it is not really "salt" they must be free of, but sodium.

> 1 tablespoon dried carrot
> 1 tablespoon dried sweet peppers
> 1 teaspoon dried parsley (see p. 216)
> ½ teaspoon celery seeds
> 1 tablespoon unrefined coarse salt
> 1 teaspoon potassium chloride

Grind the carrots, peppers, parsley, and celery seeds until all is fine. Add the salt and grind, still at high speed, until the desired texture. When ground, add the potassium chloride (which is already ground), and mix in by blending at low speed.

Store in a small jar with a tight lid.

Yield: a large shakerful.

## ONION SALT

Onion Salt is very good over meat or eggs or fish. The onion called for has been dried in rather largish chunks, but any dehydrated onion will do.

> *2 rounded tablespoons dried onion*
> *1 rounded tablespoon unrefined coarse salt*

Measure the onion and salt into the blender and process at high speed until fine. If the onion has any moisture in it at all, some of the mixture will have to be scraped from the sides of the blender with a rubber spatula.

Store in a small jar, tightly sealed.

Yield: ½ shakerful.

# DESSERTS

Desserts can be just as good for you and your family as a bowl of spinach (especially if the dessert *has* spinach in it —see Spinach Torte-Pudding, page 161). And they are an easy way to get yourself or the rest of your family into healthy foods. Serve Strawberry Ice, for example, and rest assured that the vitamin A is still in it when you serve it. Serve a Date Torte and no one is going to believe it's healthy.

Desserts fit themselves readily to blender fixing: even many "haute cuisine" recipes call for chopped nuts or fruit. And, in some of these desserts, nut flours take the place of grain flour.

## ICES

These are, probably, the simplest desserts in the book. We made dinner for a sick friend and her family, at their apartment, and invented an Ice for them on the spot, in their blender, with what their refrigerator held. They were amazed that anything that tasty could come together that quickly.

You'll see that all the Ices recipes have a certain similarity of technique: the most liquid ingredient goes in first, then any flavoring or sweetener, then any milk powder, then the ice cubes. This means that once you master the technique, you can invent any Ice that strikes your fancy—even vegetable Ices, which we didn't have the guts to include (but imagine a Cucumber-Dill Ice).

Any blender should grind ice fine enough for these ices. Here's how: drop a few ice cubes into the liquid mixture and turn the blender on at high speed (which makes a terrible racket). When half ground, add a few more cubes, pushing them down with your spatula, then blending again at high speed. Stop when the racket stops, and push down with the spatula again. Add more cubes, and repeat the process until the mixture in your blender looks almost solid.

The texture of the Ices will be more liquid than the ices you buy. However, a few hours in the freezer will solidify our homemade Ices to the point where they are in texture just like the commercial kinds. But you can serve them at once if you wish. Certainly *we* always serve Ices immediately, then store the leftovers—if there are any. But Ices made without milk will generally harden into actual ice if left more than a few hours in the freezer.

Most of these recipes make about 2 or 2½ cups—enough for 4 servings. But they make up so quickly that there is no problem about preparing seconds.

If you are using honey for a sweetener, do remember to put in the honey *before* the ice cubes. Ice causes honey to congeal, that doesn't harm the honey, but it means the honey will not mix into the liquid. If you have forgotten the honey and have already put in most or all of your ice cubes, switch to maple syrup for sweetening. Maple syrup isn't quite as sweet as honey, but it will mix well when cold.

Always keep extra cubes handy; you can never be sure that our measurements are identical, and besides, ice cubes are difficult to measure by the cup—large cubes mean less ice in a cup, small cubes fill more of the empty spaces and mean more ice.

## BANANA-MINT ICE

Use ripe, sweet bananas for this recipe. In fact, the over-ripe bananas that look too dark and soft to use for any-thing but cooking are just fine. The amount of maple syrup you use will depend on the sweetness of your bananas and on your taste. Start out with 1 tablespoon of syrup and then add more—if it needs it—after you've finished the ice crushing.

> ½ pound ripe bananas
> 1 or 2 tablespoons maple syrup
> 1 scant teaspoon dry mint leaves (see p. 216)
> about 3 cups ice cubes

Break the bananas into pieces and liquify at high speed. Add 1 tablespoon maple syrup and the mint leaves and blend. Grind the ice cubes (see page 142). Taste for addi-tional maple syrup.
Serve immediately or harden in the freezer for 2 hours.
Yield: almost 3 cups.

## BLACKBERRY-YOGHURT ICE

This recipe calls for blackberries, but there's no reason why you can't use blueberries instead. If you want to substitute strawberries, you'll probably want to increase the honey by a teaspoon.
This Blackberry-Yoghurt Ice comes out a bit tart, which is grand for adults, but for kids you might want to make it with 2 tablespoons of honey.

> ½ cup fresh yoghurt (see p. 215)
> 1 cup blackberries
> 1 tablespoon honey
> 1½ cups ice cubes

Measure the yoghurt into your blender container. Wash the berries well (if your berries are from the supermarket, wash them in *hot* water), and add to the yoghurt. Add the honey. Blend briefly, on and off several times until the mixture is fairly uniform. (You don't want to heat the yoghurt, that's why you blend briefly.) Add the ice cubes and crush as described on page 142.
Serve immediately or store in the freezer.
Yield: a bit more than 2 cups.

## CAROB MILK ICE

Milk powder can go into almost any of these Ice recipes, if you want to raise the protein and calcium level. This Ice will pass for chocolate among your children—and even among your adults. You could use any other liquid instead of the water here, but if it is orange pulp (as we use in later recipes) the liquid won't take as many ice cubes.

> ½ cup water
> 1 very heaping tablespoon noninstant milk powder
> 1 tablespoon honey
> ¼ cup carob powder
> 2½-3 cups ice cubes

Add the water, milk powder, honey, and carob powder to the blender and mix at low speed until smooth (scrape the powder off the sides of the container). Grind the ice cubes as directed on page 142.
Let this one harden for an hour or so in the freezer before serving.
Yield: about 2½ cups.

## CANTALOUPE ICE

You can substitute an appropriate chunk of Persian or Cranshaw melon in this recipe, but honeydew melon would be last choice. Any orange or yellow melon has vitamin A, while honeydew, which has a delicious sweet flavor, has none. The same holds true for yellow and white peaches. The yellow peaches have good amounts of vitamin A, while the white have not.

> ½ small cantaloupe melon
> 1 tablespoon honey
> 1 teaspoon dried mint leaves (see p. 216)
> 2-2½ cups ice cubes

Scrape out the seeds from the melon and spoon the flesh out into your blender container. Blend at high speed until liquified. Add the honey and mint leaves and blend at low until well mixed. Crush the ice cubes (see page 142).
Serve at once or store in the freezer.
Yield: almost 2 cups.

## CANTALOUPE-MILK ICE

This Ice, which is a dieter's friend because it has absolutely no addtional sweetening, comes out very much like ice cream. Also, it stores well in the freezer beyond the few hours needed to harden it. There is the protein and calcium of a pint of milk in this recipe.

> ½ large cantaloupe
> 2 very heaping tablespoons noninstant milk powder
> 2 cups ice cubes

Spoon the cantaloupe meat out into the blender container and blend at high speed until liquified. Blend in the milk powder at low speed. Add and crush the ice cubes as on page 142.
Serve immediately or store in the freezer. This Ice is even better after being stored for a day.
Yield: about 2½ cups.

## MAPLE MILK ICE

This ice calls for pure maple syrup. And, as we said earlier, that most likely does not include what you are putting on your griddle cakes (see MAIN COURSES). In commercial maple-flavored syrups today the amount of real maple syrup ranges from little to none—with the slack being taken up with corn syrup, fillers, and flavorings, which falls pretty far from anything we would recommend. The pure maple syrup we use comes from New Hampshire, but Vermont, New York State, and Canada also have excellent maple syrups. Again, it is a matter of reading labels.
This dish is unusually delicious, and nutritious.

> ½ cup pure maple syrup
> 1 very heaping tablespoon noninstant milk powder
> 2-2½ cups ice cubes

Measure the syrup and milk powder into the blender container and blend at low speed until smooth. Add the ice cubes and crush as given on page 142.
Serve immediately or harden in the freezer.
Yield: less than 2 cups.

## SOUR LEMON ICE

"Sour" is a relative word. What's neutral to us may be sour to you. Since honey is used as sweetener in this recipe you can't taste the finished Ice and then adjust with honey (as you can with maple syrup). So, taste the honey-lemon mixture before adding the ice cubes, remembering that the mixture will be very much diluted. We use the whole lemon except for seeds and skins. Peel a lemon, then cut it across the equator, so to speak, to pick out the seeds. Lemons often have seeds throughout, so make a few cuts. Then just dump the peeled pieces into the blender. The size of the pieces doesn't matter.

*3 small lemons*
*2 tablespoons honey*
*2 cups ice cubes*

Wash, peel, and seed the lemons, then drop them into the blender container and liquify at high speed. Add the honey and mix (and taste). Add the ice cubes and crush (see page 142).
Serve at once or store in the freezer for no more than 3 hours.
Yield: less than 2 cups.

## SOUR LIME ICE

If you haven't cooked with limes, beware, because they are sour, which is why we dilute them with an orange. The orange is pitted the same way as the lemon described in the previous recipe, except that oranges tend to have most of their pits visible when you cut across the equator. Do try to use a juicy orange.

*2 small limes*
*1 small orange*
*2 tablespoons honey*
*2 cups ice cubes*

Wash the fruit, then peel and pit, and liquify at high speed. Blend in the honey and crush in the ice cubes (see page 142).
Serve immediately or allow to harden in the freezer for a couple of hours.
Yield: 2 cups.

## STRAWBERRY ICE

This recipe calls for frozen strawberries, but you can freeze your own. Just wash and trim the berries, then drain and freeze in plastic bags in 1 cup lots. We use frozen berries here because with them it takes fewer ice cubes to reach a satisfactory Ice texture, leaving the flavor more intense. Don't delete the orange—without its liquid you'll have trouble blending the berries.

> *1 medium orange*
> *1 cup frozen strawberries*
> *1 cup of ice cubes (about)*

Wash, peel, and pit the orange, then liquify it at high speed in your blender. Add the frozen strawberries a few at a time with the machine going at medium speed, until they are blended. Add in the ice cubes and crush as described on page 142.
Serve immediately or harden for a few hours in the freezer.
Yield: about 2 cups.

## FRESH PEACH MILK ICE

This has a great, delicate flavor. And, with all that milk powder, it has as much calcium and protein as a pint of milk. But don't think of this as a healthy treat—think of it as peach ice cream—almost.

> *½ pound yellow peaches*
> *2 very heaping tablespoons noninstant milk powder*
> *2 rounded tablespoons maple syrup*
> *3-4 cups ice cubes*

Wash the peaches. Pit over the blender container to catch the juice. Blend at high speed for a few seconds until liquid. Add the milk powder and syrup and blend at low speed until smooth. Add a cup or so of cubes, then add more cubes and continue to blend. Keep forcing in cubes until quite thick.

Serve immediately or store in the freezer compartment.
Yield: almost 4 cups.

# SHERBETS

These Sherbet recipes are more complicated than ices and
take much longer to make. But they come out with such
interesting flavors and textures that they are well worth
the effort, and they will go a long way toward converting
your resident ice-cream addict to a healthier diet.
When you put these Sherbets in the freezer to set, don't
pour all of the recipe into 1 container: that would double
the setting time.

## UNCOOKED BLACKBERRY SHERBET

Don't think the 1¼ pounds of berries called for is an odd
amount; that's the weight of the bags of frozen berries one
finds all year round now, and also the weight of a quart
of fresh berries—so you can use fresh without any adjust-
ments.
Reduce the honey to ¾ cup if you don't like sweet
sherbet.

> ½ lemon
> 1¼ pounds frozen blackberries
> 1 envelope or 1 tablespoon unflavored gelatin
>     powder
> ½ cup cold water
> 1 cup honey
> 1 cup water (additional)
> 2 very heaping tablespoons noninstant milk powder

Wash, peel, and seed the lemon, drop it into the blender,
and liquify at high speed. Leave it in the blender container
and pour in the frozen berries but do not process. In a
saucepan, dissolve the gelatin in the ½ cup cold water,

stirring till it disappears, then add the honey. Heat, stirring, until the mixture is smooth and hot, but do not allow to boil. Pour the hot honey-gelatin mixture slowly over the berries in the blender. Blend at low speed until smooth. Pour the mixture off into a large bowl. DO NOT WASH THE BLENDER. Measure 1 cup water into the blender and add the milk powder. Blend at low speed for a few seconds until the milk is made, then pour it into the bowl with the berries. Stir well. Pour into 2 or 3 plastic containers and put in your freezer until set, perhaps 2 or 3 hours.

Yield: more than a quart.

## BLUEBERRY SHERBET

This is a double-threat dessert. You see, our freezer is very slow, and sherbet normally won't set for us in less than 5 or 6 hours. So we invented this one to be set, even in our freezer, in an hour or so. It's the double helping of gelatin that does it, making it a gelled dessert even before it is set like a Sherbet. So, you can eat it like a gelatin pudding or wait for it to harden. Either way it's delicious.

>    ½ fresh lemon peel
>    1¼ pounds blueberries
>    1 cup honey
>    ½ cup cold water
>    2 tablespoons or packets unflavored gelatin powder
>    1 cup water (additional)
>    2 very heaping tablespoons noninstant milk powder

Cut the peel into pieces and blender-grate at high speed until tiny. Put peel in a pot with the berries and honey and cook for a few minutes, no more. Dissolve the gelatin in the ½ cup cold water, shut the flame off under the berry mixture, and stir in the gelatin. Allow to cool for 20 to 30 minutes. While the berries are cooling, make up the milk powder and water in the blender. (Don't worry about those leftover bits of lemon peel still in the blender—everything is going to the same place.) Pour the milk into a large

bowl. When cooled, pour the berry mixture into the blender and blend briefly at low speed. Add to the milk, stir, and pour off into 2 or 3 plastic containers and put in the freezer to set.
Yield: almost 5 cups.

For a CHERRY SHERBET use the same recipe, substituting a bag of frozen, pitted cherries, and reduce the honey to ¾ cup.

## CRANBERRY SHERBET

The cranberry flavor in this sherbet is so deliciously un-usual that it's well worth the bit of extra preparation it requires. Of course, we use no canned or prepared cran-berries here, only the fresh ones in season (or frozen, if you can find them). But since cranberry season now ex-tends from November to March, that gives us plenty of time to enjoy them.

> 1 pound cranberries
> 1 cup water
> 1 envelope or 1 tablespoon unflavored gelatin
>     powder
> ¼ cup cold water (additional)
> 1½ cups honey
> 1 large orange
> 2 cups water (additional)
> 4 very heaping tablespoons noninstant powdered milk

Wash the cranberries well in hot water and remove any stems. In a 2-quart pot, boil berries in 1 cup of water until they pop, about 5 minutes of boiling. Dissolve the gelatin in the ¼ cup cold water and add to the cranberries (with the flame off). Add the honey, stir well, and allow to cool. Wash, peel, and pit the orange, and liquify in the blender at high speed. When the berry mixture is cool enough not to burn your finger, pour into the blender, and blend at low speed until smooth. (This fills our 5-cup container, so if yours is smaller, you may want to do it in 2 parts.) Return the blended mixture to the same pot. DO NOT WASH THE BLENDER. Make up the milk powder with the 2 cups of water at low speed. Pour into the pot and stir. The mixture will very likely curdle. Return to the blender 2 cups at a time and blend until smooth again.

For quick freezing pour off 1-1½ inches of sherbet into plastic containers and put in your freezer until set.

Yield: almost ½ gallon.

## STRAWBERRY SHERBET

This recipe is uncooked, and so all the vitamin A is intact. It's pretty fast, too. Try it with other berries.

> *1 lemon*
> *1 cup honey*
> *1 quart strawberries*
> *2 egg whites*

Wash and peel the lemon. Grate the rind in the blender at high speed until quite fine. Remove the seeds and add the lemon pulp to the blender; liquify, at high speed. Add the honey and blend until smooth. Drop the berries through the cap a few at a time, with the motor at medium speed, until all blended and smooth.

Beat the egg whites very stiff (with an egg beater, wire whisk, or electric mixer) and gently pour the mixture over them. Fold in carefully. Pour into plastic containers and put in freezer until set.

Yield: more than a quart.

# PUDDINGS

In the general food world, puddings are made with corn-starch or gelatin as thickeners, and cooked. These Puddings are not. They are all simple, quick and easy to prepare, uncooked, and as tasty or tastier than any commercial varieties.

Any of these recipes can be added to (there's not much to take away from them), or changed in any way to suit your own taste: for example, you might want to make your Banana Pudding with a tablespoon of carob powder. Also, any Pudding is a Pie Filling, too. So do use them with the Pie-Crust recipes (pages 157 and 158).

## APPLE PUDDING OR PIE FILLING

Apples are not the easiest thing to chop in a blender; here's how we do it: wash and core the apple and cut it into eighths, then turn the machine on at medium speed and drop the pieces through the hole in the blender top. The first pieces will chop quite coarse and the subsequent pieces finer (you want them fine). Drop the chunks right onto the blades, and when they begin to get stuck, stop, scrape out into a bowl, and start over.

>    *1 small lemon*
>    *1½ teaspoons cinnamon*
>    *1⅛ pounds mackintosh apples*
>    *2 tablespoons honey*

Wash and pit the lemon, cut it into quarters, drop it into the blender, and grind (skin and all) at high speed until reduced to quite small bits. Add the cinnamon, but don't process. Scrub (but do not peel), core, and cut the apples into eighths. Drop the pieces a few at a time through the opening in the blender cap, with the machine going at medium speed. When no more will blend, scrape out into a bowl and process the rest of the apples in the same way and add them to the bowl. (You *may* need a third processing to finish all the apples.) Add the honey to the bowl, and stir well.
Serve in bowls or use as a pie filling.
Yield: 4 good helpings of pudding or the filling for one 8-inch pie crust.

## PEACH PUDDING

Peaches won't blend quite thin enough for a juice or nectar (unless you like to eat your nectars with a spoon), but, like apples, they blend into a deliciously creamy sauce.

> 1 pound yellow peaches
> ½ cup walnut meats
> ¼ cup sesame seeds

Wash the peaches and pit them over the blender (to catch the juice). Blend at high speed until liquified. Measure in the nuts and seeds and stir with your rubber spatula. Blend very briefly at low speed, stir again, and blend briefly again, to chop the nuts coarsely.
Yield: about 2 cups, or filling for one 8-inch pie crust.

## APPLE PINEAPPLE PUDDING

We had to try this combination because the words sounded so good together. Actually, the fruits go rather well together, too. Use only ripe pineapples.

> 1 small lemon
> 1 pound apples
> ¾ pound pineapple meat
> ¾ teaspoon cinnamon
> 2 tablespoons dried mint leaves (see p. 216)
> 2 tablespoons honey

Scrub, pit, and quarter the lemon, drop it into the blender (skin and all), and process at high speed until ground small. Wash and core, but do not peel, the apples and cut into eighths. Process at medium speed in 2 batches until chopped. Scrape the apple-lemon mixture into a bowl.
Cut the pineapple meat (about half a medium-small pineapple) into approximately 1-inch cubes. Drop the cubes through the cap opening and process at medium speed until liquid. Add the mint leaves and cinnamon, process

again briefly, then scrape into the apple-lemon mixture. Add the honey and stir well.
For variation, stir in ½ cup coarsely chopped nutmeats.
Yield: 5 good helpings or filling for one 8-inch pie.

## BANANA PUDDING

This recipe calls for 4 small bananas, but what we actually want is about 1½ cups of banana mush (what you get after blending the bananas), so don't hesitate to add banana if it doesn't come up to that level. Banana Puddings tend to dry somewhat as they stand, so if you want this thicker for a pie filling, just let it stay in the refrigerator for a few hours before using. It is most important that the bananas be ripe.

>   *4 small bananas*
>   *½ cup nutmeats*

Break the bananas into chunks and drop into the blender container with the motor at medium speed, grinding until you have a mush. Add the nutmeats, stir in with your spatula, and grind again, briefly, until the nuts are coarsely chopped.
Yield: 2 cups.

## BANANA-COCONUT PUDDING

Very tropical. The hardest part of this recipe is getting the coconut meat out of the shell. Use fresh coconut. The fresh has a good deal of liquid in the meat, the dessicated, none, which would change the balance.

>   *meat of ¼ coconut*
>   *2 medium bananas*

Cut the coconut meat into 1-inch pieces and drop through the blender top, with the motor going at high speed. This

should yield about 1 cup of shredded coconut. Add the bananas, also in pieces, and process at medium speed until all is well blended.
Yield: about 2 cups.

## BANANA-PINEAPPLE PUDDING

There are different kinds of dried pineapple on the market, so watch out: one kind is just plain sun-dried pineapple and that is fine, but another kind is pineapple dipped in so-called "raw" sugar, and that is a no-no.

*1 pound bananas, weighed with skins on*
*1 teaspoon dried mint leaves (see p. 216)*
*½ cup dried pineapple*
*½ cup nutmeats*

Peel the bananas and break them into chunks, drop them through the cap of the blender, and blend to a mush at medium speed. Add the mint. Break the pineapple up into 1-inch pieces, pour into the blender, and process briefly at medium speed. Add the nutmeats and blend briefly until coarsely chopped.
Yield: almost 2½ cups.

# NUT CRUSTS

There is nothing intrinsically unhealthy about pies—it's just that commercial pies are made with sugared fillings and hard-shortening crusts, and even most home recipes go along the same unhealthy lines. So, here are two recipes for healthy crusts, to be used with any of the preceding recipes for Puddings or with any fruit filling.

## NUT WHOLE WHEAT CRUST

The potassium chloride called for in this recipe is a salt substitute. But more than that, it is a salt balancer, ameliorating some of the harmful effects of excess salt in our systems. By the way, in case you missed it elsewhere, don't blanch almonds.

> ½ cup almond nutmeats
> ½ cup whole wheat pastry flour
> dash sea salt
> dash potassium chloride
> 2 tablespoons liquid vegetable oil
> 1 tablespoon honey

Blender grind the almonds at high speed until they are a fine flour (you may have to help them along with your spatula—brushing nuts away from the sides of the container and onto the blades), and pour off into a bowl. Add the flour to the bowl and blend by hand. Add the rest of the ingredients and mix well. Press by hand into a 9-inch pie plate until quite thin.
This crust will require about 15 minutes baking time in a preheated medium oven.
Yield: one 9-inch crust.

## NO-BAKE CRUST

This crust is ready to eat as soon as you mix it, but it is sticky. You have to ease it out of the pie plate gently (unless you have one of those pie plates with an attachment for loosening the bottom crust). Our favorite use for this crust is in individual little pudding-pies, pressing the crust into 4 or 5 individual pudding dishes. As you see, there is no grain flour in this recipe, and no oil.

>   *1 cup nutmeats*
>   *1 cup sesame seeds*
>   *4 tablespoons honey (approximately)*

Blender grind nuts and seeds separately at lowest possible speeds, until a fine flour. Pour into a large bowl as each is finished. Add the honey (you will need less than 4 tablespoons if the nuts and seeds have expressed any considerable amount of oil). Press into individual pudding bowls or into a 9-inch pie plate.
Yield: one 9-inch pie crust, or 4 to 5 individual servings.

# TORTES

Tortes are great stuff. If you haven't ever tried them, either because they seemed too complicated or used unhealthy ingredients, here's your chance.
These are basically European—Viennese actually—we don't know of an American equivalent. The Viennese are as proud of their tortes as the French are of their mousses, and with good cause. Tortes are light and sweet, crunchy and delicious. They are certainly among our favorite desserts, and they'll be among yours, too, if you don't let yourself get scared off.

## DATE TORTE

All parents have their favorite children, and this is certainly one of ours. It has to be tasted to be believed—no description does it justice. And yet it's healthful.

*1 cup nutmeats*
*3 egg yolks*
*1/3 cup honey*
*¼ teaspoon sea salt*
*1 cup pitted dates*
*3 tablespoons whole wheat flour*
*3 egg whites*
*butter for greasing*

Blender-chop the nuts coarsely at medium speed and reserve in a large bowl. Separate the egg yolks into the blender container and the whites into another bowl (the bowl must be big enough for whipping them). Add the honey to the yolks, and blend until mixed. Add the salt. With the machine going at medium speed, add the dates, a few at a time, until they are chopped, then scrape the mixture into the bowl with the nuts. Stir together and add the flour; stir again until fairly uniform.

Beat the egg whites with a beater until they are quite stiff. Scrape the whites out onto the date-nut mixture and *cut* in thoroughly. (This cutting process is like folding, but you use only the sharp edge of the spatula. The egg-white bubbles are what rises this dish, and if you use the flat of your spatula you break a lot of these bubbles. Cutting takes longer than folding, but it's safer.)

Grease a 9" by 2" ring mold (or 2 smaller sized molds) and gently scrape the Torte batter in. Set in a cold oven, with the flame at its highest for 5 minutes, then reduce the heat to moderate. Cook for about 30 minutes altogether.

When done, turn out and eat hot or cold.

## CARROT-WALNUT TORTE

What? A Torte with vitamin A? You bet. There's no reason why any vegetables can't go into desserts.

> 1½ cups walnut nutmeats
> 1 cup carrot pieces
> ½ cup Barbados molasses
> 4 egg yolks
> 1 very heaping tablespoon noninstant milk powder
> 4 tablespoons whole wheat flour
> ¼ teaspoon sea salt
> 4 egg whites
> butter for greasing

Blender chop the nuts coarsely at medium speed and re-serve in a large bowl. Cut the scrubbed carrots into 1-inch pieces and drop through the blender top to chop at high speed. Reserve in the same bowl. Measure into the con-tainer the molasses, egg yolks (the whites go into a bowl for beating), milk powder, flour, and salt. Blend until smooth, then pour over the nuts and carrots. Mix well. Beat the egg whites (not in the blender) until very stiff. Scrape out over the nut-carrot mixture and cut in thoroughly as described on page 159.

Grease a 9-inch ring mold and scrape the batter into it. Set in a cold oven with the heat at highest temperature for 5 minutes, then reduce the heat to moderate. Bake for a total of about 30 minutes.

Turn out and eat hot or cold.

## HIGH-PROTEIN TORTE

One of the reasons this Torte is high in protein is because it contains soy flour instead of wheat flour, and soy flour is higher in protein than wheat flour.

The figs we use are not those very dry ones you find on a string. Ours (unsulfured) come from our health food co-op and are moist and soft, halfway between fresh figs and the dessicated stuff in the supermarkets.

> *1 cup walnut meats*
> *3 egg yolks*
> *⅜ cup honey*
> *2 tablespoons water*
> *¼ teaspoon sea salt*
> *1 very heaping tablespoon noninstant milk powder*
> *8 large dried figs*
> *3 tablespoons soy flour*
> *3 egg whites*
> *butter for greasing*
> *12 pecan halves*

Blender chop the walnuts at medium speed until coarse, then reserve in a large bowl. Separate the egg yolks into the blender container (reserve the whites for whipping), and add the honey, water, salt, and milk powder. Cut the figs in halves and drop through the blender top until coarsely chopped at high speed. Scrape out the mixture over the nuts and add the flour. Stir well. Beat the egg whites in their bowl until very stiff. Gently scrape out over batter and cut in thoroughly (see page 159 for cutting in).

Grease a 9-inch ring mold and scrape the batter into it. Place the pecan halves evenly around the top. Set in a cold oven, and bake with the heat at highest, for 5 minutes, then reduce the heat to moderate and bake for 25 minutes more.

Turn out and serve hot or cold.

## SPINACH TORTE-PUDDING

This recipe is not really a Torte, but it's very like a Torte, so why not include it here. Besides, there's something very appealing about a Spinach Torte—it sounds like a contradiction in terms.

*2 cups almond nutmeats*
*4 egg yolks*
*1/3 cup blackstrap molasses*
*1/3 cup honey*
*½ pound fresh spinach*
*1 cup raisins*
*4 tablespoons soy flour*
*4 egg whites*
*sesame seeds*

Blender chop the almonds coarsely, at high speed, 1 cup at a time, and reserve in a large bowl. Separate the egg yolks into the blender (reserve the whites for beating), and add the molasses and honey. Wash and trim the hard ends off the spinach. Put in a colander to drain some of the water off, but don't towel dry; the recipe needs some of that water. Feed the spinach leaves and stems into the blender 1 or 2 at a time (it takes a very little while), increasing motor speed as needed. When all the spinach is blended, add the raisins and blend very briefly. Scrape out over the nuts, add the flour, and mix well. Beat the egg whites until very stiff, carefully scrape out of the bowl over the batter, and cut in thoroughly as described on page 159. Scrape the mixture into an ungreased 9-inch ring mold, level off, and sprinkle with a handful of sesame seeds. Put in a cold oven with the heat set at high. After five minutes reduces the heat to moderate and bake an additional 30 minutes.

Do not *turn* out, *spoon* out of the mold. Eat hot or cold.

# MOUSSES

These traditional uncooked French desserts are real show-stoppers, guaranteed to get compliments from any company—or any family. And they are quite simple and nutritious.

## FRENCH CAROB MOUSSE

Here's a Mousse that's a French Chocolate Mousse in every respect—except that it has no chocolate. But even with carob, it's very French.
If you are making it for children, you may wish to use whole milk.

> 4 egg yolks
> ½ cup carob powder
> 1/3 cup reconstituted milk
> 1 teaspoon vanilla (see p. 215)
> 4 egg whites

Blend the egg yolks, carob, milk, and vanilla for about 30 seconds at low speed. In a bowl, beat the egg whites till quite stiff. Fold the blender mixture into the whites and spoon into 5 or 6 cups. Set in the refrigerator or eat at once.
Yield: 5 or 6 servings.

## ADULT MOUSSE

This is a dessert *not* for the kiddies. It's flavor is definite, and the rum is something they don't need.

> 3 egg yolks
> 3 ounces carob powder (about ⅜ cup)
> 4 tablespoons rum or brandy
> 1 cup water
> 1 very heaping tablespoon noninstant milk powder
> 1 tablespoon or 1 envelope unflavored gelatin
>    powder
> ½ cup plus 2 tablespoons strong coffee or coffee
>    substitute
> 3 egg whites

Blend the egg yolks, carob, rum, water, and milk powder at low speed until smooth. Stir the gelatin into the coffee

and then heat just to the boil. Add this mixture to the blender and beat at low speed for 1 minute. In a separate bowl, beat the egg whites until stiff. Scrape the blender mixture out over the whites and fold in thoroughly. Spoon into serving cups (we like custard cups) and place in your freezer for about an hour or until set, and then move to the fridge until served.
Yield: 6 generous portions.

## ALMOND-CAROB MOUSSE

Did you know that carob contains pectin, an aid to digestion?
Taste this recipe after adding each tablespoon of honey—it makes up sweet, and you may want to reduce the amount of honey.

> 3 egg yolks
> ½ cup carob powder
> 1/3 cup reconstituted milk
> 1 teaspoon almond extract
> 3 tablespoons honey
> 3 egg whites
> 4 almonds

Blend the egg yolks, carob, milk, almond extract, and honey at medium speed for about 30 seconds. In a separate bowl, beat the whites until very stiff. Scrape the blender mixture over the whites and fold in well but gently. Spoon into 4 cups. Cut up the almonds and sprinkle 1 over each cup.
Chill in the refrigerator or eat at once.
Yield: 4 generous servings.

## STRAWBERRY MOUSSE

The berries should be very sweet and very fresh.

½ *small lemon*
*pint strawberries*
*3 egg yolks*
*2½ tablespoons honey*
*3 egg whites*

Wash and peel the lemon. Cut the peel into strips and blender chop at high speed until quite tiny. Seed the lemon pulp and add that to the blender, processing at high speed until liquified. At medium speed, drop the berries through the container top 1 at a time until liquid. Add the egg yolks and honey, and blend at low speed until smooth. In a separate bowl, beat the egg whites until quite stiff. Fold the berry mixture into the whites gently and completely. Spoon into individual cups. Serve immediately or refrigerate.
Yield: 4 or 5 cups.

# MISCELLANY

## WALNUT SOUFFLÉ

There is another Soufflé in the book, Spinach Soufflé in MAIN COURSES.
Soufflés are really just hot Mousses. This Walnut Soufflé is one that has delighted our students and was a successful first effort for people who had never made a Soufflé, so don't you back off.

½ *-inch square fresh lemon rind*
¾ *cup walnut meats*
*3 egg yolks*
¼ *cup honey*
½ *teaspoon vanilla (see p. 215)*
⅛ *teaspoon sea salt*
*1 rounded teaspoon raw wheat germ*
*3 egg whites*

Set the oven to preheat to 325.°

Drop a ½-inch square of fresh washed lemon rind through the blender top with the motor going at high speed. Add the walnuts and chop to a coarse meal. Reserve both in a large bowl. DO NOT WASH THE BLENDER. Put the egg yolks, honey, vanilla, salt, and wheat germ into the container, and blend until smooth. Pour over the nuts and mix well.

With an egg beater, whisk, or electric beater, beat the egg whites until very stiff. Fold the batter into the whites, but not completely: leave a little marbling effect. Scrape gently into an ungreased 1½ quart casserole.

Set the casserole in 2 inches of water in your oven (we use a Dutch oven to hold the water) and bake for 45 to 55 minutes at 325°.

Do not test—look: The center will look liquid if not done. To serve, spoon out gently as soon as it's done.

Yield: 4 servings.

## BLUEBERRY APPLESAUCE

This and the following recipe are unusually creamy, no-cook Applesauces, a pleasant change from the cooked kinds, and richer in vitamins.

> 2 small oranges
> 2 tablespoons honey
> 1 pint blueberries
> 2 medium apples

Wash, peel, and seed the oranges and drop them into the blender container; blend at high speed until liquified. Add the honey and blend in. Wash the berries in hot water and then liquify in the mixture. Scrub the apples and core (but do not peel) them, then cut into eighths. Drop the chunks into the blender 1 or 2 at a time, with the motor at high speed, until all are blended. You may have to help the apples along with your spatula.

Yield: 6 servings.

## CRANBERRY APPLESAUCE

This dessert is sweet with no additional sweetener.

> 2 small oranges
> 1 cup cranberries
> 2 medium-large apples

Wash, peel, and pit the oranges, then liquify in the blender at high speed. Wash the cranberries in hot water and pick out any stems. Add to the blender container and liquify at high speed. Scrub and core, but do not peel, the apples, then cut into eighths. With the motor going at high speed, drop in a few chunks at a time until all are blended and smooth.
Yield: 4 to 5 servings.

## DATE-SEED TANNIES

These aren't dark enough to be brownies, but they're good enough to have at any time—and they are made without grain flour.

> 1 cup sesame seeds
> 2 eggs
> 1 cup (packed) pitted dates
> butter for greasing
> sesame seeds (additional)

Blender grind 1 cup sesame seeds into a fine meal, helping with the spatula when needed. Reserve in a bowl. Break the eggs into the blender and drop in the dates, with motor at medium speed; blend until finely chopped. Add to the sesame meal and mix well. Pour into a greased 7-inch loaf pan, level, and sprinkle the top with a handful of sesame seeds. Bake at medium heat for 30 to 35 minutes. To serve, cut into 12 squares, in the pan.

## SESAME-WALNUT COOKIES

With cookies this fast and easy to make, who would ever buy store-made?
Again, these cookies are made without grain flour. There is a warning here, though. They are very quick to scorch (we have eaten many a scorched Sesame-Walnut Cookie), so if your nose tells you they are getting done, even if it's less than the 15 minutes called for—check. Don't be stubborn.

> *2 cups walnut meats*
> *2 eggs*
> *1 cup sesame seeds*
> *¼ cup honey*
> *butter for greasing*

One cup at a time, at high speed, blender grind the walnuts into a fine flour and scrape into a bowl. Add the remaining ingredients to the bowl and stir well. Spoon tablespoonfuls of the batter onto a lightly greased cookie sheet, and starting in a cold oven bake at medium for 15 to 20 minutes.
Yield: about 30 cookies.

## BLENDER DESSERT CREPES

In the normal course of Crepes making, recipes call for the batter to be left standing for upwards of 2 hours, to allow the flour to "expand"—to absorb all the liquid it can. The whirling of the blender can accomplish this in 30 seconds.

> *3 eggs*
> *1 tablespoon vegetable oil*
> *1 tablespoon honey*
> *¾ cup water*
> *1 heaping tablespoon noninstant milk powder*
> *¾ cup flour*
> *½ teaspoon vanilla (see p. 215)*

Put all the ingredients into the blender and process at medium speed for 30 seconds, stopping to scrape down any flour or milk powder that sticks to the sides. For cooking instructions, see Wheat Germ Crepes on page 78.

To serve these Crepes, spread with carob and honey, or cinnamon and honey, or use to wrap around any honey-jam recipe.

Yield: about 12 Crepes.

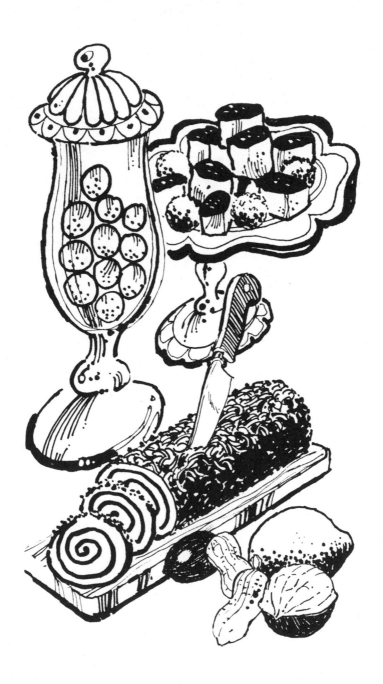

# CANDY

We have friends in Philadelphia who are into healthy foods. In fact, she, the mother of two, makes wheat germ cookies for her children. But the kids both go out and buy mallomars.

We have friends in New Jersey who have nothing but healthy foods in their house. But their children spend their allowances on penny candy.

"Why?" they ask.

The answer is simple enough. The wheat germ cookies taste of wheat germ, and the healthy foods, while nutritious, exclude sweets. And children need sweets. Their palates are more sensitive to sweets than the palates of adults.

There is nothing wrong with sweets. Does that sound heretical? Think again. There is nothing wrong with sweets —nature abounds in sweets: honey, sweet fruits, sweet nuts, sweet vegetables.

What *is* wrong is the *commercial* sweets that the kids are buying: the marshmallow cookies, the chocolate bars, the sugar candies, the soda pop.

Refined sugar is not only cavity-causing and an empty non-food, but, since it is all carbohydrates and carbohydrates require B vitamins to be processed, refined sugar draws B vitamins from your system.

Chocolate is not only a frequent allergen, but it contains

oxalic acid, which hinders calcium absorption. So children, who have the greatest need for calcium, suffer most because of all the chocolate they eat.

Commercial cakes and cookies are made with low-protein flours "enriched" with only a few of the cheapest vitamins and iron. These highly refined white flours require, like white sugar, B vitamins robbed from the body, in order to process them.

Soda pop is a special enemy of ours. Do you or your children have a lot of cavities? Don't switch your toothpaste, get off soda, especially the colas. Have you ever seen how colas can dissolve paint? That's no joke. Think of what it can do, and does, to your tooth enamel. And notice how a child will cry for a coke—if that's not addiction, what is it?

Fortunately, there is something you can do about the situation. If your kids can get sweet, delicious candy at home, they won't go out and buy junk. And that's what this chapter is about. There is no contradiction between "healthy food" and "candy." Candy, like any other food, is as wholesome as the ingredients you put in it. These candies are first of all delicious, and then, without question, nutritious. While all of them are high in carbohydrates, they contain more than enough B vitamins for their own processing without robbing your system. Also, they are rich in other vitamins and minerals and protein from wheat germ, bran, milk, soy flour and so on.

At the end of the chapter, there are a group of unsweetened candies (or perhaps they should be called "naturally sweet") for those who must restrict honey in their diet. More adult palates will enjoy these.


Let's anticipate some of the processing problems with the ingredients we use in this chapter.

COCONUT. Use only fresh coconut, except for the few instances when *dessicated* coconut is called for. We know that means that you have to break open the shell and drain the milk (a very rich liquid), and cut out the meat, and then grind it in the blender—but if you buy ready-ground *moist* coconut you are taking a chance. The coconut oil might be rancid. The best way of avoiding this is to buy a fresh coconut and break it open, grinding it as you need it, and refrigerating the unused part. Coconut is chopped like carrots. Cut the meat into about 1-inch-square pieces and drop the pieces through the hole in the cap of the blender, with the blender going at a high speed. If there are any larger pieces left you can grind them again (or eat them, they make a nice treat for the cook).

RAISINS. Any raisin is fine, so long as it's seedless, unsprayed, and unbleached. Don't allow raisins to chop down to a paste. Rather, blend only ½ cup at a time and only until most of the raisins are in bits.

DATES. For munching we prefer the domestic California dates. They are larger and have a milder flavor. But for candies, the stronger-tasting imported dates are often better. Usually we drop the dates into the blender 1 or 2 at a time (blending no more than ½ cup at one go), and allow them to blend right into a paste. This is what gives cohesion to several of our candies. Dates are tough to clean out of a blender. Try to do them last.

FIGS. Cut figs in half and treat like dates, above.

SEEDS. Poppy seeds, sunflower seeds, and sesame seeds all get treated similarly. You can put as much as a cup at a time into the blender, then grind them down at high speed until they are a fine meal. You may have to stick your spatula in along the sides of the container and help the seeds down to the blades. Also, you may have to shut off the machine and stir everything up with the spatula.

NUTS. We use nuts in three different ways in this chapter: coarsely chopped, coarse meal, and fine meal (which can be almost as fine as flour). For coarsely chopped, flick the blender on and off very briefly a few times. For coarse meal, flick it on and off very briefly a few more times. For a fine meal, treat the nuts like seeds, above.

## MAPLE-NUT BALLS

Maple syrup doesn't have the stickiness of honey, though it has more in the way of minerals. Don't squeeze the balls after they are made—they will come apart. We use three different walnut entries in this recipe: don't let it throw you. Directions for processing nuts are on page 173.

> 1 cup walnut meats (for coarse chopping)
> ½ cup walnut meats (for coarse meal)
> 2 tablespoons maple syrup (approximately)
> ½ cup walnut nutmeats (for fine meal)

Coarsely grind 1 cup walnuts into chunks at low speed. Pour into a bowl. Grind another ½ cup walnuts at medium speed into a coarse meal. Add to the bowl. Drip in maple syrup—up to 2 tablespoons—until the mixture shows cohesion. Grind another ½ cup walnuts at high speed into a fine meal. Pour onto a dinner plate. With a teaspoon, scoop out bits of the nut-syrup mixture. Shape into balls and then roll in the walnut meal.
Yield: about 16 balls.

## HALVAH

This Middle Eastern speciality is today commercially made with chemicals and a lot of other ingredients the old Turks never heard of. Eliminating the chemicals, our texture will be a little smoother, but the flavor is fine. We use unhulled sesame seeds only, because the oil in sesame seeds is very quick to go rancid once the hulls are off. That hull is perfectly edible. Read all the instructions first.

> 1 cup unhulled sesame seeds
> 2 tablespoons honey
> 1 tablespoon carob powder (optional)
> 1 teaspoon vanilla (optional)

For the basic, unflavored Halvah, begin by grinding the sesame seeds past the meal stage into a kind of nut butter. (Any seed or nut will form a butter: just keep blending it at high speed until its own oil is expressed.) Scrape out into a bowl and dribble in 2 tablespoons honey. Mix well until you get one sticky mass. If you want a more "choco-latey" Halvah, mix in 1 tablespoon carob powder (don't mix it in well—allow it to marble the candy). For a more vanilla flavor, add 1 teaspoon vanilla with the honey.

Line a small (about 4- by 3-inch) box with waxed paper and press in the mixture. Put into the refrigerator to chill for an hour or so, take out, and slice into cubes.

Yield: about a dozen 1-inch cubes.

## POPPY DELIGHT BALLS

Since all hot spices are an irritant to the stomach lining, if you have any digestive problems at all, omit the ginger.

> *1 cup poppy seeds*
> *1 cup walnut meats*
> *⅛ teaspoon ground ginger*
> *¼ cup honey*

Blender grind the poppy seeds well at high speed and scrape into a large bowl. Chop the walnuts very coarsely. Scrape half the walnuts into the bowl with the ground poppy seeds, and half onto a dinner plate (for rolling). Add the ginger and honey to the bowl and stir very well. The mass should be cohesive and handleable. Tear off walnut-sized chunks of the sticky Candy and roll and press in the nuts on the dinner plate. Round off the balls and stand them on a piece of wax paper.

Yield: about 16 big candies.

## ANTI-CHOLESTEROL POPPY CANDY

It's both the lecithin and the safflower oil that makes this Candy anti-cholesterol. The lecithin contains choline and inositol, agents in breaking down fat deposits, and the unsaturated oil is necessary to combat fat deposits.

> ½ rind of small lemon
> 1 cup poppy seeds
> ¾ cup almond nutmeats
> ½ cup wheat raw germ
> ½ cup lecithin granules
> ½ cup honey
> ¼ cup cold-pressed safflower oil

Grind the lemon rind at high speed, but don't clean it out of the blender. Add the poppy seeds, grind well at high speed, and reserve in a large bowl. Grind the almonds to a coarse meal. Add the remaining ingredients and the almonds to the bowl. Mix well until uniform.

You can eat this Candy now, rolled into balls, or you can spoon the whole batch onto a piece of waxed paper and roll it into a log for freezing and later slicing. To roll, spoon the candy onto a 1-foot-square piece of waxed paper. Wet your hands, and form the candy into a rough log shape. Roll the paper around it until the shape is smoother. Twist up the ends, and put in the freezer to harden for a few hours. Then remove, take off the paper, and slice into rounds.

## TWO-SEED BALLS

This one has a nice tart lemony taste—if you like lemon.

> 1 cup sesame seeds
> 1 cup poppy seeds (for grinding)
> ½ small lemon
> ½ cup honey
> 1 cup poppy seeds (for rolling)

Grind the seeds individually into fine meals, at high speed, and reserve in a large bowl. Liquify the washed, peeled, and pitted lemon and add to the seeds. Add the honey to the bowl and mix well. Pour the additional poppy seeds (whole) onto a flat dinner plate.

Shape bits of the Candy into 1-inch balls and roll the balls in the whole poppy seeds, setting them on waxed paper or a dish.

If you don't like lemon, try the same Candy with half a washed, peeled, and pitted orange.

Yield: about 48 1-inch balls.

## OAT CUISINE

Oats are a good food, though not as high in protein as wheat. If you really like cardamom (a favorite spice in India) use 3 pods instead of 2.

This is the only dry Candy we include.

> 2 cardamom pods
> 2 cups rolled oats
> ½ cup almond nutmeats
> 1 small apple
> ¼ cup honey

Turn your blender on high and drop the 2 cardamom pods through the opening in the cover (and then cover it). Allow to run for about 30 seconds, or until the pods and their seeds are chopped. Add the oats and process at medium speed for a few seconds. You want it mostly chopped, but not a powder. Reserve in a large bowl. Blender chop the almonds into a coarse meal and add to the bowl. Wash and core the apple, but leave the skin on. Cut into sixteenths and feed through the top of the blender a few at a time at low speed. Add the honey and continue to process for a few seconds longer, then add this mixture to the bowl. Mix well.

Lay a sheet of waxed paper on a cookie or baking sheet and scrape the mixture onto the paper. Press the mass flat with your fingers until about ¼-inch thick. Allow to dry overnight in the refrigerator, then cut into pieces and allow to dry further. If really dry, you can store in a jar. If still damp, return the uneaten pieces to the refrigerator or spread them out to dry further.

## COCONUT FRUIT CUBES

This recipe requires no additional sweetener. Don't pack the coconut when you measure it, but do pack the dates and raisins.

> *1 cup fresh-ground coconut*
> *¾ cup raisins*
> *¾ cup pitted dates*

Directions for processing fresh coconut, raisins, and dates are on pages 172–173.

Blend the ingredients individually in the order given (the dates are very sticky) at high speed. Mix well in a bowl, and shape into ¾-inch cubes.

Yield: about 16 cubes. Serve immediately or refrigerate.

## COCONUT-NUT CUBES

This is so simple.
You can substitute almonds or pecans for the walnuts if you like.

> 1 cup fresh coconut (see p. 172)
> 1 cup walnut meats
> 1 tablespoon honey

Blender grate the coconut, then the walnuts into a coarse meal. Mix in a bowl with the honey, and shape into ¾-inch cubes.
Yield: about 16 cubes.

## COCONUT-NUT CUBES II

For a sweetner-free variant, try it this way.

> 1 cup fresh coconut
> 1 cup peanuts
> 1 tablespoon cold-pressed vegetable oil
> 1 teaspoon ground star anise (see p. 216)

Blender grate the fresh coconut, then the peanuts into a coarse meal. Mix in a bowl with the vegetable oil and star anise, and shape into ¾-inch cubes.
Yield: about 16 cubes.

## COCONUT, FRUIT, AND NUT BALLS

One large coconut will yield about 4 cups of ground coconut, so you might as well try all of these coconut recipes.

*1 cup fresh coconut (see p. 172)*
*1 cup walnut meats*
*1 cup almond meats*
*1 cup raisins*
*1 cup pitted dates*
*½ cup lecithin granules*

Blender grind the coconut and reserve in a bowl. Coarsely chop the walnuts by flicking the blender on and off briefly a few times at high speed; add them to the bowl. Chop the almonds into a fine meal, and add to the bowl; coarsely chop the raisins and blend the dates to a paste (½ cup at a time); then scrape into the bowl. Add the lecithin granules and stir until uniform. Form into 1-inch balls. Yield: more than 50 balls.

## CAROB-NUT BARS

These bars come very close to commercial chocolate bars in taste and texture. Of course, without the molds you can't make them *look* like those bars, except for color. But if you or some member of your family is hooked on Hershey's, this is the chance to kick the habit. And that's not even mentioning the high nutritive value of the extra milk powder, the carob, and the anti-cholesterol quality of the lecithin.

For children, remember, you can use whole milk (see page 209).

*¾ cup reconstituted noninstant skim milk, or bottled skim milk*
*1 very heaping tablespoon noninstant milk powder*
*½ cup carob*
*2 teaspoons vanilla (see p. 215)*
*¼ cup almond nutmeats*

Add the first 4 ingredients to the blender container and blend at a high speed until fairly smooth. (You'll want to scrape the milk powder off the sides.) When smooth, add the almonds and blend briefly, still at high speed, until they are chopped to coarse bits. Scrape the mixture onto a large, ungreased baking sheet, and even it out to about ¼ to ⅜ inch thick. Don't try to make it absolutely level— it's not worth the effort.

Now the Candy must be dried. Turn a burner of your stove on high and hold the corners of the baking sheet with pot holders. Pass the baking sheet back and forth over the heat, very close to it, rotating the sheet to get at all parts, for about 3 minutes. Don't get burned. Set the baking sheet in a warmish place to set further. Within a few hours you will be able to cut it into strips and scrape it up. Do eat it within a day or so or this candy will dry out.

## CAROB CANDY BARS

For those of you who don't like nuts and vanilla, here's a very simple and plain bar.

For children, make this recipe with whole certified raw milk instead of skim milk.

> ½ cup reconstituted noninstant skim milk or bottled
>   skim milk
> 2 very heaping tablespoons lecithin granules
> ½ cup carob powder

Blend all the ingredients at high speed until fairly smooth, then proceed as in the previous recipe.

## HIGH PROTEIN SOFTEES

We hope it's not too late to warn you to grind seeds only as you need them. Though whole seeds keep well, seed meals go rancid quickly.

Here's a Candy that not only tastes good, but is also quite high in good quality protein. If you don't have maple syrup, substitute honey.

*1 cup walnut meats*
*1 cup sunflower seeds*
*½ cup raw cashews*
*1 medium apple*
*½ cup soy flour*
*½ cup noninstant milk powder*
*¼ cup maple syrup*

At high speed grind the walnuts into a coarse meal, and spread on a flat dinner plate. At high speed, separately, grind the sunflower seeds to a fine meal, then the cashews to a fine meal, reserving them together in a large bowl. Wash, core and chunk, but do not peel, the apple. Grind it at medium speed as fine as it will blend (which is not very fine), and add to the bowl. Mix in the remaining ingredients and stir until fairly uniform.
Spoon out tablespoonfuls of the mixture and drop onto the walnuts and roll until covered and round. These are very soft, so don't press, just roll. Have some extra walnuts around, just in case you need more meal for rolling. Put the rolled balls on a dish, and let them set overnight to harden slightly, then refrigerate.
Yield: about 30 balls.

## FRUIT AND NUT BARS

This is one of our favorites, and close to those fruit and nut bars you can buy in health food stores—but, of course, so much fresher

*1 cup any nutmeats*
*½ cup raisins*
*6 whole large dried figs*
*1 cup pitted dates*
*½ cup desiccated coconut shreds*

Blender chop, at high speed, 1 cup nuts into coarse bits, and reserve in a large bowl. Chop the raisins, and reserve in the same bowl. Drop the figs into the blender, at high speed, one at a time, until they reach a pastelike consistency, and reserve in the same bowl. Repeat with the dates, ½ cup at a time, and add to the bowl. Mix very well. Pour the dessicated coconut onto a flat plate.

Scoop out heaping tablespoons of the Candy, and shape into flat bars, approximately 2 x 1 x ⅜ inches, and press into the coconut.

Yield: about 16 great bars.

## SPROUT CANDY

These bars have to be eaten immediately or refrigerated, because the bean sprouts will go bad rather quickly in the open air. If you think bean sprouts are not a fit ingredient for Candy, wait until you taste this. Any bean sprouts will do, though we mostly use the old reliable mung beans.

*½ cup walnut meats*
*1 cup almond nutmeats*
*1 cup fresh bean sprouts*
*1 cup pitted dates*

At high speed, grind the walnuts into a fine meal and reserve on a flat plate for rolling. Grind the almonds into a coarse meal and pour off into a bowl. Pour the sprouts through the opening in your blender top, with the motor still at high speed, and shut off when the last sprout is poured in, then add to the bowl. Blend the dates to a paste, ½ cup at a time, then scrape into the bowl. Mix well.

Scoop out walnut-sized bits of the mixture and shape them into finger-thick little logs, then roll in the walnut meal. Refrigerate or eat at once.

Yield: about eighteen 2-inch logs.

## BANANA CANDY

Here's one that's very simple. It will dry if left in the air overnight because the raisins absorb the liquid.

> 1 banana
> 1 cup raisins
> ½ cup desiccated coconut

Break the banana into 1-inch pieces and blend at high speed with the raisins, until the raisins are well chopped. Scrape into a bowl and allow to sit for a few hours until the mixture can be handled. When dry enough, spoon out bits, shape into 1 to 1½-inch balls, and roll in the coconut. Yield: about a dozen balls.

## BANANA-NUT CANDY

This unsweetened Candy has a tart flavor from the pineapple and sesame seeds.

> 1½ cups any nutmeats
> 2 medium-small bananas
> 1 cup dried pineapple chunks
> ½ cup sesame seeds (for chopping)
> ½ cup sesame seeds (for rolling)

Grind the nuts, at low speed, into a coarse meal, and scrape out into a bowl. Break the bananas into 1-inch pieces, and blend the pineapple chunks and bananas together until the pineapple is in tiny bits. Scrape into the bowl. Chop ½ cup sesame seeds for a few seconds (you don't want a paste). Add to the bowl. Mix well. Pour ½ cup whole sesame seeds onto a dinner plate, spoon out the mixture, and roll into logs or 1½-inch balls, coating them with the seeds.
Yield: 16 balls.

# DIETETIC CANDY

This next group of Candies is designed to be acceptable to those who must restrict their intake of sugars. But that doesn't mean that people who *are* allowed honey and dates won't like them too—though they do tend to be less sweet. We hope that you won't skip them just because they are primarily for special diets.

## CAROB-CARROT CANDY

This candy is not only low in sugar, but high in protein and vitamins.

> ½ cup sunflower seeds
> ½ cup walnut meats (for fine meal)
> ½ cup walnut meats (for chopping)
> 1¼ cup carrots
> ½ cup noninstant milk powder
> ¼ cup carob powder

At high speed, grind the seeds and ½ cup walnuts, separately, into fine meal, and scrape into a large bowl. Chop the second ½ cup of nut coarsely (flick the blender on and off a few times), and add to the bowl. Scrub and trim, but do not peel, enough carrots to make 1¼ cups when cut into 1-inch bits. Blend at high speed by dropping 1 or 2 bits at a time through the opening in the blender top (keep your hand over the opening—the flakes tend to fly), and scrape into the bowl. Stir the milk powder and carob together before adding to the bowl.
Mix together well, and scrape out onto an 18-inch piece of waxed paper. Shape into a roll about 9 by 2 inches (see page 176 for rolling instructions), and put into your freezer until it hardens. Slice to serve.
Yield: about 1 pound of Candy.

## COCONUT CAROB ROLL

The coconut water called for in this recipe comes, free, with the coconut. It's a mild but pleasant drink by itself, so drink whatever you don't use in candy making. A large coconut yields about 1 cup of liquid.

Bran is the outer coating of the wheat berry. It has high-quality protein and B vitamins.

> 1 cup fresh coconut
> ¼ cup carob powder
> ½ cup bran
> ¼ cup coconut water

Grind the fresh coconut according to instructions on page 173. Blender mix all the ingredients toegther well, into an airy mass. Scrape out onto a 12-inch piece of waxed paper and roll tightly. (See page 176 for rolling.)

Set into the freezer and allow to harden before slicing.

Yield: one 6 by 1½ inch roll.

## COCONUT APPLE CANDY

Apples make a good natural sweetener. You should try them in other recipes calling for small amounts of sugar or honey if you have to restrict your sugar intake.

> ¾ cup any nutmeats
> 1 cup fresh coconut
> ½ medium apple
> dash or two cinnamon
> 1 tablespoon raw wheat germ

Coarsely chop the nutmeats and reserve in a large bowl. Shred the coconut (see p. 173) and add it to the bowl; wash and core, but do not peel, the apple, cut into chunks, and blend as fine as it will chop, then add to the bowl. Sprinkle the cinnamon and wheat germ over the surface and mix well.

Shape into ¾-inch balls and set on a plate or waxed paper.
Refrigerate what isn't eaten at once.
Yield: about 24 balls.

# 8

# BEVERAGES

Some folks think that the only use for a blender with beverages is to reconstitute frozen orange juice. Some others, more health sophisticated, think its only use is to reconstitute their powdered noninstant milk. Both are quite wrong. We enjoy a broad spectrum of drinks from our blender—including a few juices that contain more vitamins than any you can squeeze out of a juicer. But don't mistake; your blender is not a juicer, and most whole fruits and vegetables won't give you a thin juice. Some will, but most will not. Another difference between your blender and a juicer is that with blended juices you eat the pulp—rich in minerals—instead of discarding it, as in a juicer.

In this section we include Juices, Nectars, Drinks, and Milks. The divisions are not all that clear: if it is all fruit and comes out thin, we've called it a Juice; if it is all fruit and comes out thickish, we've called it a Nectar; if it has water added, it's a Drink; and if it contains milk or looks like milk—you've guessed it, Milk.

Although we have recipes for concentrates to store in the refrigerator, there's no way to prevent vitamin loss during storage. So, as a general rule, drink your beverages when you make them.

# JUICES AND NECTARS

There are some fruits that blend out quite thin, without any real preparation beyond removing a rind, while others are thick; some require sweetening, and some are fine quite straight. We'll mention some of the plain juices in this section, even though 1 ingredient hardly makes a recipe, because you just may not have thought of them as blenderable.

To prepare oranges quickly, first peel and then cut across the equator. All the pits will be visible for picking out.

Lemons can be done the same way; but often lemon pits are distributed more throughout the fruit. Make the central cut, and then make a horizontal cut through each half.

To get the pulp from a grapefruit, cut across the equator and pit, and then spoon the flesh out. Really give the grapefruit a scraping, but avoid the white middle rind; it is very bitter.

Wash all fruit and vegetables well, even though we don't always use the rind in the recipe. They are all sprayed and you can get spray on the flesh of the fruit by cutting or handling. Especially, wash cranberries in hot water. There are no unsprayed commercial cranberries, and we do eat the skin.

## WATERMELON JUICE

Here's a natural. Weigh the melon with the rind on.

*1 pound melon*

Cut the melon from the rind, and pit. Break into 1 to 2-inch pieces. Blend at lowest speed.
Yield: 9 to 10 ounces of juice.

## GRAPEFRUIT JUICE

*1 medium-sized grapefruit*

Wash, pit, and scrape out the grapefruit as described on page 190. Blend at low speed until all liquid.
Yield: about 1 cup of juice.

## CANTALOUPE JUICE

Any of the melons will make juice, so judge by these proportions. Remember, the yellow and red melons are rich in vitamin A while the white and greenish melons are not. So honeydew is sweeter (and higher in calories) but cantaloupe is healthier– and usually cheaper.

*½ medium cantaloupe*

Spoon the seeds out of ½ cantaloupe and then spoon the flesh into the blender. Blend at medium speed until liquid.
Yield: about 1 cup.

## GRAPE JUICE

This one really varies with the grape you use. Almeria grapes, available in the spring, don't yield as much juice per cup of grapes as do Riebier grapes. Seedless grapes yield more yet. But any grape will give you juice—and the sweeter the grape, the sweeter the juice.

*2 cups grapes*

Wash the grapes well (especially imported grapes—apart from whatever spraying they get in the field, they are sprayed on entry to this country), and remove from their stems. Blend at low speed briefly (so as not to blend the seeds), until the pulp is liquid. Pour through a strainer set in a bowl, and when most of the liquid has strained out, *press* the pulp against the strainer until you've gotten out as much as will come.

If you don't mind chewing your juice a little, do not strain when you use seedless grapes. But, in that case, blend for a full 15 seconds.

Yield: ¾ to 1½ cups, depending on the grape.

## TOMATO JUICEY

Well, the truth of the matter is that tomato doesn't really make a juice in the blender. It makes something *like* a juice (hence, Juicey), but thicker than a canned or bottled tomato juice—and without the added salt present in commercial tomato juices.

> 1 pint cherry tomatoes
> or
> 1 pound ripe tomatoes
> 1 teaspoon granulated kelp

Wash and trim the tomatoes, pour into the blender, and liquify at high speed. Add the kelp and blend until smooth.
Yield: about 1½ cups.

## UNSWEETENED GRAPEFRUIT-ORANGE JUICE

Bioflavonoids are beneficial substances present in the white underskin of citrus fruit. In this juice we use the white of the orange.

> 1 grapefruit
> 3 medium oranges

Wash, pit, and scoop the pulp out of the grapefruit; wash, pit, and peel the oranges. Blend at high speed until liquified.

(This juice can be diluted with ½ cup water.)
Yield: about 20 ounces.

## BANANA-GRAPEFRUIT JUICE

Bananas are very flavorful when ripe, so bypass those spot-less yellow-green ones or let them ripen. Bananas are useful for making any combination thicker and sweeter.

> *1 grapefruit*
> *1 medium banana*

Seed and pulp the grapefruit as described on page 190. Blend at low speed until the pulp is liquified. Peel the banana and break into 1-inch chunks. Add to the blender and process at medium speed until smooth.
Yield: 1½ cups.

## CREAMY WATERMELON-STRAWBERRY NECTAR

Both watermelon and strawberries are high in vitamin A, which makes them nutritionally a good buy whenever they are available. You don't do anything to make this drink creamy—the strawberries take care of that.

> *1 pound watermelon*
> *½ cup fresh strawberries*

Spoon the watermelon off the rind and pick out the seeds. Dump the pitted spoonfuls in the blender. Wash and trim the berries, and add to the melon. Blend at medium speed until smooth and creamy. Taste.
If the juice isn't sweet enough (sometimes strawberries are quite tart), add 1 tablespoon of honey.
Yield: more than 1 cup.

## GRAPEFRUIT NECTAR

The dates not only sweeten the grapefruit in this recipe but they add a delightful, though subtle, flavor. Make sure you pit the dates before you blend them. We know from experience that blended date pits are troublesome to the teeth.

    *2 grapefruits*
    *4 pitted dates*

Wash, seed, and pulp the grapefruits as described on page 190. Blend at low speed until all the pulp is liquid. Add the dates and blend at high speed until processed in.
Yield: 2 cups.

## ORANGE-CRANBERRY NECTAR

The season for cranberries is all too short. So, when this low calorie, very tasty fruit is available in the fall and winter, put a couple of boxes into your freezing compartment. Cranberries require no blanching or pretreatment and maintain good texture for about 3 months.

    *6 small oranges*
    *½ cup cranberries*

Wash, peel, and seed the oranges as described on page 190. Put into the blender and process at high speed until liquified. Wash the cranberries well in hot water. Add them and blend at high speed until smooth.
Yield: 2 cups of Nectar.

For an ORANGE CRANBERRY COOLER, blend 2 tablespoons honey into the Nectar and store in the refrigerator. When wanted, dilute with 2 parts water to 1 part Nectar.

## GRAPEFRUIT-CANTALOUPE JUICE

This is a combination that has to be tasted—it can't be described.

> ½ cantaloupe
> 1 grapefruit

Seed the melon and spoon out the flesh into the blender. Process at high speed until liquified. Wash, seed, and pulp the grapefruit as described on page 190, and spoon the flesh into the blender. Blend at low until smooth. Yield: 2 cups.

# DRINKS

## ORANGEADE

When the commercial makers market orange juice, a great deal of the oil from the skin is included. It's not intentional, but the squeezing process cannot help pressing the skin, which expresses this bitter oil. When you peel an orange, leaving on some of the white, and then blend it, you get all the nutrients the orange has to offer, without the bitter oil.

> 3 small oranges
> 2 tablespoons honey
> 6 medium-small ice cubes
> 1 cup cold water

Wash, peel, and pit the oranges as described on page 190 and put the flesh into the blender container. Blend at highest speed until liquified. Add the honey and blend in. (Do *not* put the ice in before the honey—ice thickens honey and makes it collect on the blades rather than blend in.) Blend in the cubes, at high speed, then blend in the water at low speed. Yield: almost 1 quart.

## APPLE-CRANBERRY DRINK

Apples make a delightful drink, but one that is quite thick. We add a cup of water here to get it to a more Drinklike consistency, but if you like a Nectar consistency, reduce the water to ½ cup.

> *1 small orange*
> *1 cup water*
> *¼ cup cranberries*
> *1 tablespoon honey*
> *1 medium apple*

Wash, peel, and pit the orange as described on page 190, and put it in the blender. Process at high speed until liquified. Add the water. Wash the cranberries well in hot water, and remove any stems, and add to the blender. Process at high speed until smooth. Add the honey. Wash and core, but do not peel, the apple; cut it into chunks, and blend at medium speed until smooth again. Yield: 2½ cups.

## MINT-A DRINK

When you use the blender, all the vitamin A of the strawberries stays available.

> *1½ cups water*
> *1 tablespoon dried mint leaves (see p. 216)*
> *1 apple*
> *½ cup cranberries*
> *½ cup strawberries*

Measure the water into your blender container. Add the mint leaves and process briefly at low speed. Wash, core, and chunk the apple (skin on), and blend at medium speed until liquid. Wash (in hot water) and pick over the cranberries and strawberries. Process at medium speed until smooth. Yield: almost 3 cups.

## MINT COOLER

Here's a really refreshing drink for a change from lemonade.

> 2 medium oranges
> 1 small lemon
> 1 teaspoon dried mint leaves (see p. 216)
> 2 tablespoons honey
> 6 ice cubes
> 1 cup water

Wash, peel, and pit the oranges and lemons as described on page 190. Put into the blender and process at high speed until liquified. Add the mint leaves and honey. Process at low speed. Add the ice cubes and blend at high speed until well chopped. Add the water and blend at low speed until smooth.
Yield: 3 cups.

## GRAPEFRUIT DRINK

We add honey and water to the grapefruit in this recipe because we use some of the bitter white and the skin which makes for a thicker mixture.

> 1 medium grapefruit
> 2 tablespoons honey
> 1 cup water

Peel the grapefruit, removing the rind and as much of the white as easily strips away. Cut in half and pick out the seeds. Drop the halves in the blender and process at high speed until liquified. Add the honey and water and blend at low speed until smooth and well distributed.
Yield: 2½ cups.

## GRAPEFRUIT-CRANBERRY DRINK

Here, again, we keep some of the bioflavonoids of the grapefruit.

>*1 grapefruit*
>*½ cup cranberries*
>*1½ cups water*
>*2-3 tablespoons honey*

Peel the grapefruit, scraping off as much of the white as conveniently comes off. Cut in half and pick out the seeds, then blend at high speed until liquified. Wash the cranberries in hot water and pick them over, add, and blend at medium speed until well chopped. Blend in the water, then 2 to 3 tablespoons honey, to taste.
Yield: 3½ cups.

## MOCK CLAM JUICE COCKTAIL

We're off clams until they clean up the coastal waters, but here's a drink reminiscent of better (or more unknowing) times.

>*½ pound tomatoes*
>*1 large stalk celery*
>*1 tablespoon granulated kelp*
>*1½ cups water*

Wash the tomatoes, cut into quarters, and blend at high speed until liquified. Wash a stalk of celery and cut into 1-inch chunks, then add and blend at high speed until well chopped. Add the kelp and the water and blend at low speed for about 5 seconds.
Yield: more than 3 cups.

## UNSWEETENED GRAPEFRUIT APPLE DRINK

Of course, Delicious is the name of the apple, not a description of its taste. If your blender has the room, try doubling the recipe.

> 1 grapefruit
> 1 Delicious apple
> ½ cup water

Wash, then pit the grapefruit as described on page 190. Spoon the pulp into the blender and process at medium speed until liquid. Wash and core, but do not peel, the apple. Cut into ¾-inch chunks, then blend at high speed until smooth. Add the water and mix at low speed for a few seconds.
Yield: 2 cups.

## FOUR-FRUIT NECTAR

Mixed fruit drinks are among the best. Fruits together have a delicious flavor, often better than any of the individual tastes.

> 2 medium oranges
> 1 small lemon
> 1 medium Delicious apple
> 3-4 dates
> 1 cup water

Peel and pit the oranges and lemon as described on page 190. Blend at high speed until liquified. Wash and core the apple, but do not peel. Cut into ¾-inch chunks and blend at high speed for a few seconds. Pit the dates and add them, processing at medium speed until the mixture is smooth. Add the water, blending at low speed for a few more seconds.
Yield: almost 3 cups.

## THICK TOMATO COCKTAIL

When you shop for tomatoes, look and feel (never mind the dirty looks from your greengrocer—it's your money). A ripe tomato is soft and deep red, not hard, firm, and pale—though this is what we've been educated to think of as a good tomato. Remember, tomatoes are picked and shipped green. What we're leading up to is this: if you are buying tomatoes from a supermarket, you might as well get the tomatoes that have been price reduced. They have been in the store only a day or two longer than the higher-priced ones, and have very little nutritional difference.

> ½ pound tomatoes
> 1 stalk celery
> 1 small green pepper
> 1 teaspoon granulated kelp
> ½ cup water

Wash and quarter the tomatoes. Blend at high speed until liquified. Wash the celery (leave on the greens) and cut into 1-inch pieces. Blend at high speed until it disappears. Wash, seed, and cube the pepper, then blend at high speed until well chopped. Add the kelp and water and blend at low speed until smooth.
Yield: about 20 ounces.

## VEGETABLE COCKTAIL

Most of us don't eat watercress, and we should—it's very rich in vitamin A and vegetable protein. In this mild drink you have an opportunity to get used to its strong flavor.
And here's a chance to use some of that cabbage water you've been saving since you made Coleslaw. (If you haven't made Coleslaw, feel free to use an unsalted vegetable cooking water.)

*1½-2 cups cabbage water*
*2 celery stalks*
*1 Kirby cucumber*
*4 stalks watercress*
*1 teaspoon granulated kelp*

Measure the water into the blender container. Wash the celery (leaves and all) and cut into 1-inch lengths. Wash and trim the cucumber (don't peel a Kirby as they are sent to market without wax); cut into ½-inch pieces. Wash the watercress. Put the three vegetables into the container with the kelp. Blend at medium speed until smooth. Yield: 2½-3 cups.

## ORANGE-BANANA NECTAR

This Nectar is quite thick and rich, despite the cup of water.

*3 small oranges*
*3 small bananas*
*1 cup water*

Wash, peel, and pit the oranges as described on page 190. Put into the blender and process at high speed until liquified. Break the bananas into 1-inch pieces and add to the oranges, blending at medium speed until smooth. Measure in the water and blend at low speed for about 5 seconds. Yield: more than 3 cups.

## BLACKSTRAP NECTAR

Here's one blackstrap molasses dish you can give even the most anti-blackstrap eater because you can't taste it. It's a fine way to get started on blackstrap. It doesn't take much of this dark molasses to give you all the copper you need to absorb your day's requirement of iron.

>1 orange
>1 cup water
>1 apple
>2 small bananas
>1 rounded tablespoon blackstrap molasses

Wash, peel, and pit the orange as described on page 190. Blend at high speed until liquid. Add the water. Wash and core, but do not peel the apple; cut it into 1-inch chunks, then blend at medium speed until smooth. Break the bananas into 1-inch pieces and blend in well. Add the molasses and blend at low speed until mixed in. Yield: 3 cups.

## ORANGE YOGHURT COCKTAIL

You should make your own yoghurt, it's so easy (see p. 215). But, if you don't make your own, at least buy in a busy store—one with a quick turnover—and choose a brand without preservatives.

>3 small oranges
>½ cup water
>¼ cup yoghurt

Wash, peel, and pit the oranges, as described on page 190. Then blend at high speed to liquify. Add the water and blend for several seconds at medium speed. Reduce the speed to low and blend in the yoghurt briefly. Yield: 2 cups.

## STRAWBERRY CRANBERRY COCKTAIL

This is a tart drink, even with the honey. So, if you like something *really* tart, leave out the honey.

1 cup strawberries
1 cup cranberries
1 cup water
2 tablespoons honey

Wash the strawberries and blend at medium speed until
liquid. Wash the cranberries well in hot water and pick
off any stems. Add with the water and blend at medium
until smooth. Blend in the honey at low speed.
Yield: 2½ cups.

## BLUEBERRY ORANGE DRINK

This drink has a marvelous color—more blue than orange,
though, because blueberries are *very* blue.

3 small oranges
1 cup blueberries
½ cup water

Wash, peel, and pit the oranges as described on page 190.
Liquify at high speed. Wash the blueberries in hot water
and pick off any stems. Add with the water and blend until
quite smooth.
Yield: about 2½ cups.

## CANTALOUPE-STRAWBERRY DRINK

A ripe cantaloupe is a soft cantaloupe, but shake the melon
before you take it home. If you can hear a lot of liquid
sloshing around inside, the chances are good that the
melon is overripe.

½ cantaloupe
½ teaspoon dried mint leaves (see p. 216)
1 cup water
1 cup strawberries
1 tablespoon honey

Seed the melon and spoon the flesh into the blender. Liquify at high speed. Add the mint leaves and water; wash the strawberries, and blend until smooth at medium speed. Blend in the honey at low speed.
Yield: 3 cups.

## LEMONADE CONCENTRATE

This Lemonade Concentrate is to be stored in the refrigerator, and then added to water as desired. We give the recipe for an amount of Concentrate for 1 quart water.
For an excellent variation (and better mineral content) substitute maple syrup for the honey.

>*4 lemons*
>*4 tablespoons honey*

Wash, peel, and pit the lemons as described on page 190. Blend at high speed until liquified. Blend in the honey at low speed.
Add 5 tablespoons of the Concentrate to 1 cup of water to serve immediately, or store in the refrigerator.

## LEMON TEA

The herb tea with which we make this recipe is toasted yerba maté. We make it as follows: boil 1 quart water, then add 1 tablespoon tea leaves and allow to steep for 15 minutes. Do not boil the tea. This herb tea has the advantage of containing no caffeine, so you can give it to the children without that fear.

>*1 lemon*
>*2 tablespoons honey*
>*3 cups strong herb tea*

Wash the lemon well, cut in half, and pit as described on page 190. Blend at high speed, peel and all, until well chopped. Add the honey and the tea and blend until uniform (the lemon bits will rise to the surface when you stop blending, but that's no worry).
Store in the refrigerator or serve over ice cubes—or both.
Yield: almost 1 quart.

# MILKS

Try these milks for variety and good nutrition.

## CASHEW MILK

Be sure you use raw cashews and not roasted cashews. The roasted nuts have had the vitamin E destroyed by the heat, as well as much of the enzymes.

>    2 cups water
>    2 tablespoons honey
>    1 cup raw cashews

Put all the ingredients in your blender container and blend for about 15 seconds at high speed to make a very smooth, uniform liquid.
Yield: about 2½ cups.

You can make a yoghurt with this recipe, but it is a thin, creamy yoghurt rather than the thick yoghurt you're used to. If you wish to make yoghurt of Cashew Milk, start with warm water. The directions for making yoghurt are on page 215.

## COCONUT-CASHEW CREAM

This recipe started out to be a Milk, but it got too rich and thick for a Milk, hence, Cream. Fresh coconut is what is called for, and the recipe won't work with any other kind. The imported dates are smaller than the domestic California kind, but they have a stronger flavor.

If this is your first cracking of the coconut, substitute the coconut water for some of the water in the recipe.

> ¼ fresh coconut
> 2 cups water
> 2 very heaping tablespoons noninstant milk powder
> ½ cup raw cashews
> 12 imported dates, pitted

Cut the coconut meat into ½-inch squares, drop through the opening in your blender top, and process at medium speed until well grated. Add the water and milk powder and blend until the milk is made up. Add the cashews and dates and blend for about 30 seconds until very smooth. Yield: more than 3 cups.

## COCONUT-DATE MILK

This Milk is thinner and more coconutty than Coconut-Cashew Cream (above). As in the previous recipe, feel free to substitute coconut water for part of the plain water.

> 1/3 fresh coconut
> 2 cups water
> 2 very heaping tablespoons noninstant milk powder
> 12 imported dates, pitted

Cut the coconut meat into ½-inch squares and drop through the opening in your blender top, a few at a time, with the machine going at medium speed. When all the coconut is grated, add the remaining ingredients and blend for about 30 seconds until smooth and even. Yield: almost 3 cups.

## LILAC MILK

Your family's acceptance of this drink depends on their sense of humor.
In the days when margarine was oleo and sold uncolored to distinguish it from butter, some friends of ours took food dye and colored their oleo deep purple, just for laughs. No one at the table could eat it. They threw it out —at a time when they couldn't afford to throw anything out. But that was a less sophisticated time, and this is lilac, not deep purple.

> *3 cups purple cabbage water (see p. 101)*
> *3 very heaping tablespoons noninstant milk powder*

Put the ingredients in the blender and blend at low speed until even.
Yield: 3¼ cups.

# BREAKFASTS
# IN A GLASS

There are commercial "liquid breakfasts" on the market—just mix the powder with milk and you get one thousand percent of your daily requirements . . . of what? Well, mostly calcium, from the milk, and chemicals, from the substitutes for nutrients.

The liquid breakfasts in this chapter—we call them Starters—are all natural, in the sense that all the nutrients come from food or food supplements (not from chemicals). Some are strong flavored, for those who are used to the taste of eating yeast; some are quite mild flavored, tasting more like a milkshake than a healthy drink.

These Starters are certainly not our everyday breakfast. We prefer a substantial breakfast and lunch, and a light dinner —so as to have maximum nutrition when we most need it, and a light meal at night. However, when rushed, these breakfasts are super.

They are especially good for the milk and the eating yeast that most contain. The calcium in the milk is excellent for the nerves (try it if you have trouble falling asleep); the yeast is an excellent source of B vitamins (the best after liver).

For children, try using "supermilk." Substitute certified raw milk for the water, *and* use the milk powder. Certified raw milk is a truly "whole" milk from inspected and certified healthy cows. It is neither pasteurized nor homogenized.

## PUSSYCAT STARTER

This is for beginners. It is mild and creamy, yet full of vitamins and minerals. You can make this starter stronger and stronger as you and your family get accustomed to the taste of eating yeast, adding a teaspoonful of the yeast at a time. Don't increase the yeast in big jumps—that's a good way to turn people off this nutritious drink.
For banana you can substitute an apple or pear—washed and cored, but not peeled.

> *1 banana*
> *2 very heaping tablespoons noninstant milk powder*
> *2 cups of cold water*
> *1 heaping tablespoon eating yeast*
> *1 tablespoon blackstrap molasses*
> *1 tablespoon honey*

Peel and break the banana into 1-inch chunks in the blender container. Add the remaining ingredients and blend at medium speed until smooth. With your spatula, scrape the yeast, milk powder, honey, or molasses that may have stuck to the sides of the container, down into the drink, and blend again until even. Serve immediately. Yield: 2 large glasses.

## BANANA-CAROB STARTER

Here's another Starter for beginners. The carob powder (carob is a digestive aid, rich in pectin) is sweet, so you need much less sweetener. As with Pussycat Starter, you can increase the eating yeast when you feel brave.

> *1 banana*
> *2 very heaping tablespoons noninstant milk powder*

*2 level tablespoons carob powder*
*1 level tablespoon eating yeast*
*2 teaspoons blackstrap molasses*

Peel the banana and break it into 1-inch pieces. Put it into the blender with the remaining ingredients and blend at medium speed until creamy. Scrape down whatever sticks to the side of the container and blend again until even. Yield: 2 large glasses.

## HIGH-CALCIUM STARTER

Dolomite is a rock. If you are a gardener you will recognize dolomite as a desirable source of limestone. For us human creatures it is a desirable source of calcium. Bone meal is another calcium source—an animal source, which, as the name states, comes from ground bones.
Dolomite (and bone meal) has no flavor of its own, and, if it is powdered or ground well, won't interfere with the flavor of anything you put it in. This means that you can add dolomite to any other starter or beverage without changing its flavor.
Each glass of this starter contains more than twice your minimum daily calcium requirement. The yoghurt aids in calcium absorption.

*1 rounded tablespoon dolomite powder (or 30 tablets*
*well ground)*
*2 very heaping tablespoons noninstant milk powder*
*2 cups water*
*1 tablespoon blackstrap molasses*
*2 heaping tablespoons yoghurt*

Measure the dolomite, milk powder, water, and molasses into the blender and process at medium speed for about 15 seconds. Add the yoghurt and blend at low speed briefly, until well mixed. Yield: about 2½ cups.

## UNSWEETENED EASY ORANGE STARTER

Here's a Starter for beginners that is quite low in calories as well as being high in B vitamins and protein.

>     2 oranges
>     1½ cups water
>     2 very heaping tablespoons noninstant milk powder
>     1 level tablespoon eating yeast

Wash and peel the oranges, cut across their equator, and pick out the seeds. Drop the 4 halves into the blender and process at high speed until liquified. Add the remaining ingredients and process at low speed until well blended, scraping whatever sticks to the sides of the container with your spatula.
Yield: about 1 foamy quart.

## TWO BY TWO CAROB STARTER

Don't think of this as you would a chocolate drink—though carob is a good substitute for chocolate. Carob is lower in calories than chocolate, it doesn't contain the allergens that so many people are sensitive to, and it has calcium and phosphorous.

>     2 cups water
>     2 very heaping tablespoons noninstant milk powder
>     2 heaping tablespoons eating yeast
>     2 heaping tablespoons carob powder
>     2 tablespoons sweetener (1 tablespoon honey and
>     1 tablespoon blackstrap molasses)

Measure the water into the blender and then add the rest of the ingredients. Blend at low speed until well mixed.
Yield: about 2½ cups.

## V-6 STARTER

Here's a nonyeast Starter that's high in most vitamins other than the B's, as well as calcium, iodine, and iron. If you want to eat it later in the day, think of it as a cold vegetable soup. All the vegetables must be washed well.

>   ½ pound tomatoes
>   ½ pound Italian green peppers
>   ¼ pound spinach
>   2 medium stalks celery
>   handful watercress
>   1 tablespoon granulated kelp
>   ½ cup cold water

Wash and quarter the tomatoes, then liquify at high speed. Seed and chunk the peppers, and blend into the tomato until liquid. Feed the spinach leaves and stems into the mixture 1 at a time until liquid. Cut the celery, with greens, into 1-inch pieces and blend. Add the watercress and kelp, and blend until smooth. Add the water and blend for about 10 seconds at low speed until well mixed. Serve at once.
Yield: about 3 cups.

## CREAMY STARTER

Most of the milk and yeast Starters are creamy, but here's one that is especially so because of the bananas, which give it a texture like a malted.

>   1 cup water
>   2 very heaping tablespoons noninstant milk powder
>   2 bananas
>   2 heaping tablespoons eating yeast
>   1 tablespoon honey

Add the water and milk powder to the blender container. Break the bananas into 1-inch pieces and drop in. Add the

yeast and blend well. Taste for the amount of honey you wish. If you've gotten used to the flavor of the yeast with other Starter recipes, perhaps you won't want any honey at all.
Yield: more than 3 cups.

# MAKE YOUR
# OWN . . .

This is a section of some blender things and some non-blender things that we use in blender cooking. They are available commercially, but here we tell you how to make them or dry them or grind them yourself.

## VANILLA

The commercial vanilla extracts you buy are mostly alcohol, so why not make your own with your own alcohol and a vanilla bean. The flavor is quite vanilla and the processing goes on in your own kitchen.

Put 1 vanilla bean in a half-pint bottle, then fill the bottle with dark rum. After about a week, the rum is infused with the vanilla bean and you can use it in any recipe calling for vanilla. Don't throw away the bean—it's re-usable.

## YOGHURT

Yoghurt is easy to make for yourself. It requires no special equipment and it's a must in any well-balanced diet.

In the blender, process at low speed 3 very heaping table-spoons of noninstant milk powder and 2 cups of water. Take a clean 1-quart jar. Pour in the milk and some yoghurt starter or ½ cup of yoghurt from a commercial brand that you like and which has no chemicals. Stir by hand and put aside at room temperature, 75° or more, for about 16 hours (about 12 hours at 95°). This should yield a yoghurt as thick and, some say, better tasting than the kind you started with.

## HERBS

There are herbs that you can grow on your windowsill, such as basil and sage; there are herbs readily available from the produce department of your local supermarket, such as parsley and dill; and there are herbs you can buy dry, but which sometimes need additional processing, such as bay leaves, seeds, and star anise.

FOR HERBS YOU GROW: Harvest throughout the season—an occasional clipping encourages most plants to further and bushier growth. Wash the herbs, and allow to drain well. When there is no free water on the leaves, put into the bottom of a paper shopping bag, then hang over a doorknob of a convenient, out of the way, door. Hanging the bag by both handles protects the herb against most dust. When dry, crumble and store in jars with tight lids.

FOR FRESH HERBS YOU BUY: Herbs bought from your greengrocer are treated in the same way, but they have to be washed thoroughly in hot water, to get rid of any insecticide or fungicide they may have been sprayed with. Dry the same way.

FOR DRY HERBS YOU BUY: Herbs such as bay leaves, dill-seed, and star anise are often the more useful in a quick blender recipe for a little grinding. For bay, grind a dozen leaves or so at a time at high speed. With dill seed, or any seed, grind a tablespoon at a time, also at high speed. For star anise (a popular herb in Oriental cooking, which includes both seeds and their star-shaped pods), grind an ounce at high speed. Store all of them in tight, small glass jars.

# GRIND YOUR OWN GRAIN

Grains begin to deteriorate as soon as they are ground; you see, the bran of a grain, the outer covering, keeps it fresher than any packaging material can.

You can have fresh-ground grains, and without a special grinder. Your blender will grind most grains to a mixture of flour and meal, appropriate for coarse bread, muffins, cookies, or cereals. For a really fine meal, you may have to process as much as a minute in the blender—and processing that long without any liquid in the container makes our blender run quite hot.

## CORN
Grind 1 cup of dried corn kernels at high speed until a meal.
Yield: about ½ cup.

## WHEAT AND RYE
One cup of wheat or rye berries ground at high speed to a fine meal/flour combination.
Yield: a little less than 1 cup.

# THE BLENDER IN YOUR GARDEN

Here are a few blender tricks that benefit our plants. Some of them we use ourselves, others come from friends.

## EGGSHELLS
Eggshells are a good source of calcium and lime for your houseplants. They also help aerate the soil. Make certain the shells are completely dry before you store them. Also, be sure you scrape the whites out of your eggshells when you cook, otherwise, not only are you wasting some of the egg, but you may get an offensive odor when you use the shells in your potting soil.
Break the dried shells into pieces and grind fine, a cup or so at a time, then store in plastic boxes. Don't inhale the dust. Use some in all your potted plants.

## PEANUT SHELLS
These are a little more difficult to blend, but they are also a welcome addition to potting soil.
Break the shells into smaller pieces, then grind fine ½ cup at a time.

## BANANA PEELS
We don't know what it is these peels have, but roses love it.
Cut the peels (minus the bananas) into 1-inch pieces and blend until almost liquid. Sprinkle around rose bushes and work into the soil.

## NUT SHELLS
These are the harder shells such as from almonds and walnuts. The blender will make terrible noises while blending them but persevere and all will come out well.
Grind a couple of cups of nut shells into a very coarse meal and scatter around the base of your rhododendrons.

# Index